Mentoring Teens

To order additional copies, please contact us.
BookSurge, LLC
www.booksurge.com
I-866-308-6235
orders@booksurge.com

Mentoring Teens

A Resource Guide

Carol L. Miller, M.Ed.

2006

Mentoring Teens

TABLE OF CONTENTS

This book is dedicated to
my nephew Casey —
Your gentle spirit and kind heart
will always be remembered.

INTRODUCTION

It's tough to be a teenager in today's world. Life has become fast-paced and complex. Family, school, and community performance expectations of young people can be overly demanding and unrealistic. Negative peer pressure continues to influence teens into rebellious, at-risk behaviors. Developmentally, teenagers are present-focused, want immediate gratification, and usually don't consider the short- and long-term consequences of their actions. They are inexperienced and in need of adult guidance. However, too many teens do not have anyone in their lives who has the time and expertise necessary to help them grow into happy responsible adults.

- Sara's mother is a single parent, working two jobs to support her three children. When Sara's mom is home, she is cooking, cleaning, and doing the best she can to keep the bills paid.
- Juan's family moved to the U.S. from El Salvador two years ago. They do not speak English well and have no experience with schools in this country. They want Juan to get a good education, but they don't know how to help him.
- Shannon has lived in nine different foster homes during the last six years. She has had five different caseworkers, all of whom have had heavy caseloads. It seems that she just gets settled into a new home and she has to move again.
- Hector's parents are both corporate professionals who often put in twelve to fourteen-hour days. They are working hard on their careers and have little time left over each week to focus on Hector's needs.
- Sofia is fourteen years old, and Arnold is sixteen. They are teen parents living on their own in a small, rundown apartment. Arnold has dropped out of school and works at a fast food job to support them. Sofia attends a school for teen parents that provides daycare for their child.

The number of teens who go through each day with limited or no guidance from a knowledgeable, concerned adult is staggering. Yet we still expect these young people to grow into responsible, hard working, contributing members of our communities and are surprised and dismayed when they disappoint us.

Fortunately, there are people who are willing to be mentors for teenagers. Some adults participate in organized mentoring programs like Partners, Inc. or Boys and Girls Club. Counselors, caseworkers, and probation officers provide guidance to adolescents as part of their job descriptions. Scout leaders, church youth counselors, coaches, family members, and other adults reach out and support young people in need of assistance. A mentor is any person who provides guidance and support for an individual who is learning skills needed to be successful in school, on the job, and in life.

Evaluations of mentoring programs for teens have shown that a mentor helps teenagers make positive changes in their lives that result in:

- Improved academic achievement,
- Increased high school graduation rates,
- Increased post-secondary education enrollment,
- Higher rates of employment,
- Improved family and peer relationships,
- Increased civic involvement, and a
- Decrease in high-risk behaviors.

Mentoring adolescents produces positive results for the entire community. The nation needs more people willing to be mentors for our teenagers, and we need to provide these individuals with resources that will help them be more effective in their mentoring roles.

Sometimes mentors do not know what to do when they are with their mentees. Mentors themselves do not have time to continually research information and develop activities that will support their mentees' goal attainment. The *Mentoring Teens: A Resource Guide* has been written to provide mentors, parents, and teenagers with an easy-to-use guide to activities and resources that will assist teens in becoming successful in life.

Unit One: Getting Started outlines the role of the mentor, discusses the five areas of human growth, and provides strategies for developing a strong mentor-mentee relationship. The unit includes information on how to involve and support the mentee's family and how to work collaboratively with school staff.

Unit Two: Self-Concept and Life Success defines self-concept and explains how social, academic, physical, and cultural self-concept impact life success. The unit explains how self-concept is developed, including the affects of adult messages, stereotypes, discrimination, and culture shock on a youth's self-esteem. Strategies for improving a teen's self-concept are outlined.

Unit Three: Communication Skills discusses the importance of communication skills — listening, speaking, reading, and writing — in everyday successful living. The unit includes activities that mentors and mentees can do together to practice and improve communication skills.

Unit Four: Study Skills provides techniques on getting ready to study, taking good class notes, reading strategies, writing and editing school papers, and taking tests.

Unit Five: Life Skills brings together information and resources on physical health, mental health, safety, relationships, decision-making, civic responsibility, and goal setting. Every section contains website listings that will provide more in-depth information on each subject.

Unit Six: After High School — Career Planning, Post-Secondary Education, and Employability Skills provides activities that guide teens through the process of choosing a career path, selecting and applying to a post-secondary school, writing a resume, and interviewing for jobs.

Mentoring Teens provides mentors with basic information, activities, and resources that will assist teens in becoming successful. Use the manual to help your interactions with your mentee be more productive; share the manual with your mentee's family; and read with your mentee about the topics that are timely to her current needs. You may not be around to observe all the positive changes you help your mentee make, but never doubt that your efforts make an important difference in his life.

UNIT ONE: GETTING STARTED

A. Role of the Mentor
    Who Is A Mentor?
    Why Is Mentoring Important?
    Goals of Mentoring
    The Mentor's Role
    Mentoring to Empower

B. The Five Areas of Human Growth
    Defining the Five Areas of Growth:
        Intellectual, Social, Emotional, Moral, Physical
    Life Success and the Five Areas of Growth

C. Establishing Mentoring Relationships
    Get Trained—Know the Rules
    Get Acquainted
    Build Trust
    Overcome Your Fears
    Identify and Build On Strengths
    Set the Boundaries
    Schedule Your Time Together

D. Including the Family
    Family's Role
    Family Structure
    Family Strengths
    Family Hospitality
    Overcoming Barriers

E. Working With Schools
    Educational Team
    School Handbook
    School Resources
    School Calendar
    Policies & Procedures
    Report Cards
    Graduation Requirements

A. ROLE OF THE MENTOR

Who Is A Mentor?

The National Mentoring Partnership describes a mentor as "a caring, adult friend who devotes time to young people to help them achieve their potential and discover their strengths." Mentors provide positive support and a commitment of time, energy, and resources to help their mentees identify and achieve their goals for the future. A mentor assists each mentee in learning and practicing the skills needed to be successful in school, on the job, and in life.

Why Is Mentoring Important?

Evaluations of mentoring programs across the country demonstrate the importance of a mentor in helping young people make positive changes in their lives. Students who have mentors have a higher high school graduation rate, improved grades and school attendance, and a significant decrease in negative behaviors.

The Search Institute identifies *40 Developmental Assets* that help young people grow up to be healthy, caring, and responsible. By being a mentor, you are providing your mentee with two of these assets:

- A young person receives *support* from three or more non-parent adults.
- Parents and other adults *model positive, responsible behavior.*

Youth most in need of an adult mentor are often lacking in the family and school support they need to be successful. Some parents may be working two or more jobs and do not have time to provide needed support, or family members may not have the skills or experience required to provide their children with needed assistance. Middle and high school teachers and counselors will have 150 or more students they see each week, making it difficult for them to provide long-term help to individual students. As the mentor, you play a vital role in helping your mentees reach their full potential and realize their goals for the future.

Mentoring Goals

The goals of mentoring are to assist a youth in increasing positive behaviors and decreasing self-destructive behaviors. These goals include:

- Increased academic achievement as measured by grades and test scores
- Increased high school graduation rates
- Increased post-secondary education enrollment
- Employment
- Good school and work attendance
- Improved self-esteem and self-confidence
- Improved family and peer relationships
- Increased civic involvement
- Improved life and social skills
  and
- Decreased or eliminated high risk behaviors: truancy, behavior problems, drug and alcohol use, violence and criminal activity, and teen pregnancy.

Mentor's Role

A Training Guide for Mentors by Jay Schmink provides the following descriptors of what a mentor is or is not:

A Mentor Is: a friend, coach, motivator, supporter, advisor, tutor, teacher, and advocate

A Mentor Is Not: a parent, social worker or professional counselor, probation officer, police officer, disciplinarian, playmate, financier, priest or minister

The primary role of a mentor is to be a *positive role model.* The youth you are mentoring will be observing you very closely. If you don't "walk your talk" and model the behaviors and skills you are trying to help your mentee learn and practice, you will not be effective.

Your role as a mentor is to:
- Build a trust relationship with your mentee;
- Be persistent in establishing and maintaining a supportive relationship with your mentee;
- Spend quality time every week with your mentee;
- Be a good listener;
- Be a non-judgmental friend;
- Serve as an advocate for your mentee;
- Maintain confidentiality unless harm may result to your mentee or others if you do not report information your mentee shares with you;
- Follow through by doing what you say you'll do;
- Maintain regular communication with your mentee;

- Be accessible and keep open the lines of communication;
- Seek assistance when you feel you are not a good match for your mentee or when your mentee's needs are more than you can handle;
- Praise and encourage your mentee through all of her growth steps;
- Be punctual and follow through;
- Follow the rules of the mentoring program, school, and family;
- Be gently honest with your mentee, her family, and teachers;
- Set respectful boundaries; do not tolerate or model foul language, bad manners, inappropriate behavior, or excessive spending of money;
- Be prepared with well-planned activities that promote personal growth;
- And again, be a good role model.

Mentoring to Empower

An effective mentor is a person who practices the principles of empowerment. Reflecting on the old adage of "Give a person a fish and they eat today; teach them to fish and they eat for a lifetime," Dunst and Trivette explain that the empowering person:

1. Assumes that a person has many competencies or the capacity to become competent.
2. Understands that a person's poor functioning is the result of a social structure or lack of resources that makes it difficult for existing competencies to operate.
3. Realizes that the person must attribute behavior changes and personal achievement as a direct result of his own actions.
4. Expects the person to play a major role in deciding what is important to him or her, setting personal goals, and determining how these goals will be achieved.

The *empowering mentor* will remember and practice the following guidelines:

- If your mentee is capable of doing something, you will provide support but will not do the act for him.
- If your mentee is capable of learning how to do something, you will assist her in developing the skills and will provide opportunities and support as she practices the skills.
- If your mentee is not capable of doing something that needs to be done to meet his needs, you will help him find and learn how to access the appropriate resources and assistance.
- You will expect your mentee to make her own decisions and point out to her that behavior changes and learned skills are a result of her decisions and efforts.
- You will allow your mentee to learn from the results of his choices and actions, being there to celebrate his achievements and help him learn from his mistakes.

B. THE FIVE AREAS OF HUMAN GROWTH

Defining the Five Areas of Growth

Children learn and grow in five major areas: intellectual, social, emotional, moral, and physical. To be successful in school, at work, and in life, your mentee will need your assistance in each of these areas.

Intellectual: Intellectual growth refers to a person's capacity for knowledge and rational thought. A person gains knowledge through reading, study, observation, and experience. Both formal education in school and on the job and informal learning taught by community and family teachers assist youth in developing intellectually.

Social: Social growth refers to a person's ability to relate well with other people. Youth must be taught social skills that are appropriate for different situations. These skills include proper manners, acceptable protocol, responsible behavior, and the role expectations of one's family, community, school, and job.

Emotional: Youth grow emotionally by learning to identify emotional responses in themselves and others and by understanding how emotions affect their own and others' behavior. Emotional growth includes the ability to communicate one's feelings and emotional needs, manage one's emotions in healthy ways, and accept responsibility for one's emotional happiness.

Moral: Youth grow morally by learning and following principles of right or wrong behavior as taught to them by their family, school, and society. Moral learning includes ethics, empathy for others, conscience development, respect, tolerance, and fairness.

Physical: Physical growth is learning how to take care of one's needs for nutrition, rest, exercise, hygiene, and health care.

Life Success and the Five Areas of Growth

Successful youth have good intellectual, social, emotional, moral, and physical aptitudes. A youth who lacks skills in any of the five areas is at risk of family problems, school failure, and difficulties on the job and in the community. The *Success in the Five Areas of Growth* chart provides examples of skills your mentee needs to learn to function well. Review this chart with your mentee. Discuss other skills you have found to be important in the five areas of growth. Notice how the five areas of growth overlap. Skills and traits that are important at home are also important at school and on the job.

Success and the Five Areas of Growth

Area of Growth	At Home	At School	On the Job	In the Community
Intellectual Growth	Manage time Follow directions Budget Fill out forms Do homework	Read Write Do math Take tests Organize work	Follow directions Read manuals Write reports Work on computers	Pass driver's test Read signs Vote Read newspaper Know the law
Social Growth	Good manners Be a good host Share with others Be helpful	Obey the rules Respect teachers Share with others Work in a group	Good customer service Teamwork Get along with supervisor Be polite	Get along with neighbors Participate in social events Help others
Emotional Growth	Able to express love and sorrow Manage anger Support others' emotional needs	Manage anger Responsible No blaming No put-downs Say "no" to negative peer pressure	Manage anger No blaming No put-downs Be nice to others No office romances	Manage anger Be nice to others Appropriate public displays of affection
Moral Growth	Respect others' privacy Be honest Help others Do the right thing	No cheating No bullying Be tolerant and accepting of others Be honest	Be honest Be tolerant and accepting of others Work hard Be responsible	Be tolerant and accepting of others Be a good citizen Volunteer Obey the laws
Physical Growth	Eat healthy meals Practice good hygiene Exercise daily Get adequate rest Don't smoke, drink or use drugs Practice safe sex	Participate in gym and sports Eat a healthy breakfast and lunch Get help for vision & hearing problems Say "no to drugs and alcohol	Take breaks to rest or exercise Use safety equipment Eat nutritious snacks & lunch Wash hands often Have a neat, well-lighted work area	Recycle Help reduce smog Pick up trash Grow plants Conserve water Turn down the TV & radio volume Avoid second-hand smoke

C. ESTABLISHING THE MENTOR/MENTEE RELATIONSHIP

Get Trained—Know the Rules

If you are signing up to be a mentor in an organized mentoring program, you must become familiar with the mentoring program rules and procedures. You will probably be asked to:

- Fill out an application
- Have an interview
- Go through a security check
- Show proof of car insurance
- Provide a copy of your driver's license

Most programs will provide you with an orientation and initial training. During this process, think about the characteristics of the youth you would like to work with such as age, gender, ethnicity, religion, area of town youth resides, family structure, special talents, personal interests, physical abilities and disabilities, gender orientation, and so forth. Sharing this information will help the program coordinator find you a mentee who will be a good match for you.

Get Acquainted

The program may provide you with personal information about your mentee before your first meeting. Use this information as conversation starters to find out more about your mentee. Spend time during your initial 2 or 3 meetings to get to know each other and talk about your interests, likes, dislikes, families, heritage, dreams, etc. Discover what you have in common, as all good relationships are based on similarities.

Build Trust

Establishing a trust relationship takes time, and some people need more time than others to develop trust in another individual—especially with someone they have never met before. It is important that both your mentee and his family learn to trust you if you are to be effective in your mentoring role. Keys to establishing trust are:

- Be non-judgmental.
- Be accepting of your mentee's and her family's beliefs and lifestyles even when they may be different from your own.

- Be respectful of the family.
- Be accepting of the family's hospitality.
- Share your own background and experiences.
- Communicate at their level, being careful not to use vocabulary they do not understand or to talk "down" to them.
- Discuss what your role is as their child's mentor.
- Keep the family informed about what you and their child will be doing.
- Ask the family's permission and follow their rules.
- Be consistent.

Your mentee and her family will learn to trust you as you demonstrate that you are reliable and follow through with your commitments.

Overcome Your Fears

The mentoring experience can produce unexpected fears. You may be introduced to cultural differences that are at first uncomfortable for you. Your mentee may live in a neighborhood that has a reputation (real or perceived) for being dangerous. You may discover that the reality of mentoring is more than you bargained for. You may get stuck in stereotypical beliefs that interfere in your relationship with your mentee. The first step is to recognize and admit your fears by being honest with yourself. Then try the following:

- Talk about your fears and feelings in a safe, supportive environment with a person who will be non-judgmental.
- Talk honestly about your fears and concerns with the program coordinator.
- Try to understand where these fears originate. Are they realistic and based on facts and actual events? Or are your fears a result of stereotypes or your discomfort in being exposed to a different cultural system?
- Learn more about your mentee's cultural heritage and family background.
- Ignore any negative gossip about your mentee's family. Form your own opinions based on your interactions with them.
- Work hard at being open to different lifestyles and belief systems. Remember, your lifestyle is not necessarily better; it's just different from theirs.
- Give yourself time to adjust. New situations become less scary once you get to know people better.
- Look for the positives. Focus on the strengths of your mentee and her family.

Identify and Build On Strengths

There is a tendency among overburdened school staff and human service providers to focus on the negative and the many problems and challenges with which they themselves and their clients must contend. This negative focus can become a block to positive change.

You may even hear someone say, "This is an impossible situation," or "There is just no helping this family." Do not allow yourself to get caught up in negative thinking. It is not helpful. Instead, actively look for the strengths of your mentee and her family.

> *The author mentored a young Latino boy from a very poor, uneducated family. It was not easy to find the strengths upon which to build the mentor-family relationship. However, the positives were there. Mom worked hard to keep her five children together, fed and clothed. The children were very close and supportive of each other. All the children treated me with respect and were appreciative of what I did for them, no matter how small or insignificant. Years later, this young man continues to call, and his family still feels connected to my husband and me. He and his sister have passed their GED and are continuing their education.*

You may not be around to observe all the positive changes you have helped him make, but never doubt that your efforts have made an important difference in the life of your mentee.

Set the Boundaries

Families have behavior expectations; classes have rules; communities have laws; workshops have norms. You will need to establish some relationship guidelines with your mentee. Only you and your mentee can decide what these guidelines and expectations will be. Consider discussing the following topics:

- Calling each other when you have to cancel.
- Getting the family's permission for the mentee to participate in activities.
- Being honest with each other.
- Maintaining confidentiality—except when a person may be in danger by not telling others what they need to know to be safe.
- Being respectful of each other and defining respectful behavior.
- Taking turns on activity choices.
- Being open to learning new things.
- As issues and concerns arise, agree to talk to each other and come to a resolution instead of shutting down and damaging the relationship.

Schedule Your Time Together

Use a time management exercise to help you and your mentee decide when you can meet. Both of you will need to write out your weekly schedules to determine when you have time available to get together. Make sure that you list school and work hours, regularly scheduled activities, family time, and homework hours. Pencil in your mentor/mentee dates and commit to making your dates a high priority. When a legitimate scheduling conflict does arise, agree to give each other as much notice as possible and find another time to meet that week.

D. INCLUDING THE FAMILY

Family's Role

A young person's family members are her first and most important teachers and support system. The family is legally and morally responsible for the youth's well-being. Children rely on their families to take care of them and help them survive in their environment. And even though adolescents may voice dismay with their parents, there is a strong bond that connects them to the family. As a mentor, you will be more effective if you establish a collaborative relationship with your mentee's family. Include the family in your activity planning discussions, ask about their concerns, share your concerns, and include them in celebrations of your mentee's progress.

Family Structure

Families come in many different shapes and sizes. The people raising your mentee may be the biological mom or dad, adoptive parents, foster parents, step-parents, grandparents, aunt, uncle, sister, brother, family friends, or court-appointed guardians.

The family structure may have cultural dynamics that you need to recognize and adapt to. For instance:

- Multiple generations and extended family members live in the home.
- The children are often home alone as their parents must work two or more jobs to financially support the family.
- Your mentee may have childcare and housekeeping responsibilities that impact your time together.
- Your mentee may live in a house, apartment, mobile home, or homeless shelter.
- The home may seem small in size for the number of people who live there.
- The family may live in a neighborhood that is unfamiliar and uncomfortable for you.
- If your cultural heritage is different from your mentee's, you may not understand the beliefs that influence the family's behaviors.

As you work with your mentee and introduce her to new experiences, remember that she will be returning to her home environment and will usually live there until she's at least eighteen years old. It is important to spend time including family members in discussions of your activities so that your mentee does not begin to feel separate and isolated from her family. Your mentee's family is her lifelong support system, whereas your role as her mentor is a temporary one.

Family Strengths

Every family member will have strengths that you need to acknowledge and appreciate. When establishing the relationship with your mentee's family, look for special talents and skills such as:

- Dad loves fishing and is good at tying flies.
- Mom makes the best green chili and tortillas.
- Brother is a good wrestler.
- Sister is an artist and loves to draw.
- Someone grows beautiful flowers.
- Everyone in the family is bilingual.

Ask them questions about their work. Tell them of similar interests and skills you or someone in your family may have. Be generous and honest with your compliments.

Family Hospitality

Good relationships are based on reciprocity. As their child's mentor, you are providing a service for the family. Allow family members to occasionally do something nice for you in return. In many cultures, it is expected that you will graciously accept the family's offers of hospitality. Sit down and eat with them when invited. Accept and openly admire gifts, such as a special drawing or a potted plant. Your acceptance of the family's hospitality demonstrates to your mentee that her family is important and special. Remember, part of your mentee's self-esteem includes pride in her family.

Overcoming Barriers

In your efforts to include the family, you may encounter the following barriers:

- The family has different goal expectations for their children. They may need them to quit school and find work to help support the family.
- The family would like their children to get a good education, but they don't understand what that involves. They don't know how much time and hard work is required; they do not understand what classes their children need to take.
- The family may not have adequate English language skills, so they are unable to communicate with school personnel. They are unable to read information sent home or express their concerns and ask questions.
- Family members do not have the academic skills needed to help their children with their homework.
- The family may not understand their role in supporting their children's education. They don't realize what their responsibilities are in providing a learning environment at home and setting expectations for academic and life success.
- The family may be operating in survival mode with all of their energy and time

being spent on feeding, clothing, and housing their family. They do not have the resources required to support their children's education.

- Family members may have had negative life experiences and are emotionally fearful or angry with the school and other societal systems.

To overcome these and other possible barriers to family inclusion, it will be important for you to stay open-minded, flexible, and non-judgmental. You may find that your role as a mentor needs to be expanded to include:

Mentoring the Family: Just as you use the *Mentoring Teens* manual with your mentee, you may need to share and explain this information to your mentee's family. Be patient and check for understanding. Simply reading this manual and other types of information to them may not be adequate. You may need to provide explanations in language that is easier for the family to comprehend.

Linking the Home with the School: As you learn the concerns of both the family and school personnel, you can assist them in communicating directly with each other. Be the mediator who facilitates the communication process, helping each side to understand the other's perspective and needs.

Providing Transportation: Your mentee's family may not have reliable transportation, money for gas, or adequate vision for night driving. If you believe it is important for family members to be present at a school activity or community event, offer to drive them in your car. Check to be sure that your mentoring program rules allow you to provide transportation. You will need to have a valid driver's license and good car insurance.

Finding Resources: The family may have basic human needs that interfere with their ability to be supportive of their children's education. As a mentor, seeking out and helping the family connect with community resources would be very helpful.

Providing Information: Families who are not familiar with secondary and post-secondary education systems in this country will benefit from information you can provide. They cannot participate in the process or make sound decisions regarding their children without this information.

Reframing the Future: The family may need your help in connecting their child's education with future goals of a good job, home ownership, and economic stability. Provide them with examples of others who studied hard and achieved these life goals by being academically successful.

Doing Whatever It Takes: Good mentors will go the extra mile, help provide or find needed resources and support for their mentees and families whenever possible, and persist in guiding their mentees towards academic and life success by doing whatever it takes.

E. WORKING WITH SCHOOLS

As a mentor, you will need to be involved with the educational process at your mentee's school. Remember that each school has its own policies and curriculum guidelines. Procedures and student expectations may have changed since you were in school. Use this section of Unit One to give you ideas on how you and your mentee's school can collaborate.

Educational Team

Your mentee's educational team members are those people who work together to help youth be academically successful. Team members include your mentee, his family, teachers, principal, counselor, specialists like an "English as a Second Language" teacher, tutors, and you—the mentor.

- Make an effort to meet the team members; let them know you are the mentor.
- Ask team members what special concerns they have about your mentee.
- Check regularly with the teachers of classes that are more difficult for your mentee.
- Find out what students are studying.
- Ask teachers for insights as to how you can be most helpful.
- Check to be sure homework is being completed and turned in to the teacher.
- Give team members your contact information and encourage them to call you when your assistance is needed.
- Keep a list of the team members' names, phone numbers, and email addresses.

School Handbook

Helpful information is available in your mentee's school handbook. Ask your mentee if you can read the handbook and then make copies of the pages that contain information you might need during the school year.

School Resources

Most high schools will have career, financial aid, scholarship, and college information available in the counseling office or career center. Encourage your mentee to make an appointment with his counselor so he can obtain college and career information. Many schools also sponsor a college night where recruiters from post-secondary institutions pass out information and answer questions about the school or university they represent. If possible, go with your mentee and her family to college night so you can be their guide and answer questions they may feel uncomfortable asking someone they don't know.

Find out what extra-curricular activities your mentee participates in. Ask her if she is on a sport's team, in music, drama, art, student government, or a cultural group. Attend her school events when they are open to the public. If she is not in any extra-curricular activities, encourage her to find an activity she might enjoy and give it a try. Remind her that participation in extra-curricular activities is a good addition to her college and scholarship applications. Research supports that students are less likely to drop out of school if they are involved in school activities.

Other school resources available to students might be the library, computer lab, health clinic, teen parent program, free or reduced lunch program, student work-study positions, and so forth. If your mentee has a particular need, help him find out if the school has resources that can assist him.

School Calendar

Keep a copy of the school calendar in your *Mentoring Teens* book. Important dates to know include:
- First and last day of school
- School holidays and vacation breaks
- End of the grading periods
- Report card delivery dates
- Testing schedule
- ACT/SAT/PSAT and Advanced Placement Test dates
- Graduation
- Special events like school dances, plays, music programs, sports

School holidays and vacation breaks are good times to schedule special activities with your mentee. Avoid scheduling activities the night before major testing dates or near the end of a grading period when final projects or exams may be due. Attend your mentee's special programs and athletic games or take them to school events in which they do not directly participate. Take your mentee to high school and college graduation ceremonies so they can visualize and anticipate their own graduation.

Policies & Procedures

School Checkout: If you are picking your mentee up at school, be sure the family has notified the office and put your name on the security clearance list. Always go to the office first. Introduce yourself and follow the sign-out procedures.

Attendance: Become familiar with the school's attendance policies. Some high schools have a policy that a certain number of tardies to a class equal an absence. After a certain number of absences, the youth can be kicked out of class and lose credit for that semester. If the class is a requirement for graduation, the youth will have to start over again and take the class the next semester or school year. Explain to your mentee the importance of attending and being on time for every class.

School Fees: School membership and participation is expensive, especially if you have more than one child in school. Your mentee's reluctance to participate in a school activity may be due to the cost involved; i.e., uniforms, equipment, travel, yearbook, class rings, letter jackets, school t-shirts and hats; activity fees, and so forth. Check with the office about fee waivers or special funds set aside to pay fees that students cannot afford. If you have the resources, consider buying your mentee a school hat or t-shirt as a birthday, Christmas, or Hanukkah gift. Help your mentee think of ways to earn the money he needs for school activities.

Report Cards

Schools send out report cards four or six times each year. In the middle of these reporting periods, some schools send home letters to inform parents that their children are failing in certain classes. Other methods used to keep parents current on their children's progress in school are telephone call-in numbers and the school's website. Check out your mentee's grades on a regular basis. Discuss strategies for improving low grades and celebrate the hard work and effort they put in to achieving good grades. A small celebration is called for even when your mentee improves a grade from an "F" to a "C."

Remind middle school and junior high students that the grades they earn in 9th through 12th grades are averaged into their grade point average for high school graduation and college entrance requirements.

Graduation Requirements

Credits for high school graduation requirements are measured in Carnegie units. In most cases, one unit is given for each year of instruction for classes that meet 5 hours a week. School districts may differ slightly in the credits required, but the basic unit requirements are:

Language Arts	4 units
Math	3 units
Social Studies	2.5 to 3 units
Science	2.5 to 3 units
Physical Education	1 to 1.5 units
Electives	Approx. 8 units
Total	22 units

You can find out what your mentee's high school graduation requirements are in the school's handbook, on the school's website, or from the counselor. Work with your mentee and his family on scheduling classes that will ensure he will be able to graduate on time. The *High School Schedule* form at the end of this section can assist your mentee in keeping track of classes taken each year.

Remember, if students fail or are dropped from a class, they do not get credit and will have to take the class again in summer school or the following school year. Encourage your mentee and his family to keep report cards in a safe place so that they will have a record of high school credit units he has earned. Check with the school counselor every year to be sure your mentee is on track with enough credits to graduate with his class.

High School Graduation Requirements

Your Mentee's School Requires	Your Mentee Has Completed
Language Arts (Usually 4 units required)	9th Grade _____ 10th Grade _____ 11th Grade _____ 12th Grade _____
Math (Usually 3 units required)	9th Grade _____ 10th Grade _____ 11th Grade _____ 12th Grade _____
Social Studies (Usually 3 units required)	9th Grade _____ 10th Grade _____ 11th Grade _____ 12th Grade _____
Science (Usually 3 units required)	9th Grade _____ 10th Grade _____ 11th Grade _____ 12th Grade _____
Physical Education (I to I.5 units)	9th Grade _____ 10th Grade _____ 11th Grade _____ 12th Grade _____
Electives (5 to 8 units)	9th Grade _____ 10th Grade _____ 11th Grade _____ 12th Grade _____

UNIT ONE: BIBLIOGRAPHY

Borba, Michele. (2005). *Building Moral Intelligence.* http://www.moralintelligence.com. (accessed on 5/18/05).

Dunst, Carl J. and Trivette, Carol M. (1987). "Enabling and Empowering Families: Conceptual and Intervention Issues," *School Psychology Review.* Volume 16, No. 4, pp. 443-456.

Healthy Communities, Healthy Youth. (2004) "40 Developmental Assets." Minneapolis, MN: Search Institute. http://www.search-institute.org/assets/assetcategories.html. (accessed on 5/20/05).

Hein, Steve. (2005). *Introduction to Emotional Intelligence.* http://equ.org/history.htm. (accessed on 5/18/05).

Miller, Carol L. and VanDecar, Elena. (2004). *Parenting for Academic Success.* Denver, CO: Latin American Research and Service Agency.

Miller, Carol L. and Torres, Noel. (1992). *Effective Family Outreach: A Training Manual.* Ft. Collins, CO: Even Start Family Centered Learning, Poudre R-1 School District.

The National Mentoring Partnership. (2005). http://www.mentoring.org. (accessed on 5/19/05).

Smink, Jay. (1999). *A Training Guide for Mentors.* Clemson, SC: National Dropout Prevention Center, Clemson University.

UNIT TWO: SELF-CONCEPT AND LIFE SUCCESS

A.   Understanding Self-Concept

   Defining Self-Concept
   How Self-Concept Is Developed
   Social, Academic, Physical and Cultural Self-Concept
   Indicators of a Positive Self-Concept

B.   Adult Messages that Impact Self-Concept Development

   Positive and Negative Adult Messages
   Effects of Stereotypes and Discrimination
   Culture Shock

C.   Building Self-Concept

   Focus on the Positive
   Praise and Encouragement
   Positive Self-Talk
   Activities that Build Self-Concept
   Remembrance Album

A. UNDERSTANDING SELF-CONCEPT

Defining Self-Concept

A person's self-concept is those beliefs you have about yourself and is based on what you think other people believe to be true about you. For example, a parent gets upset with his child's behavior and yells, "You are so stupid!" The parent does not really believe the child is stupid and is only reacting out of frustration with the child's behavior. However, the child may internalize her parent's label, delivered at high volume, and begin to believe that she is 'stupid'.

Whether or not a person's self-image is accurate, the individual lives her life as if it were true. In her book, *From Rage to Hope,* Kuykendall states, "It is the development of a child's self-image that is perhaps the most important barometer in assessing probability of future success." Self-concept forms the foundation that will determine a youth's level of confidence, motivation, willingness to take safe risks, and decisions he makes for himself throughout his life.

How Self-Concept Is Developed

A youth's self-concept develops and changes over time based on the feedback she receives from significant people in her life. These people can be family members, teachers, ministers or priests, coaches, youth group leaders, peers, and you—the mentor. Feedback messages are how we let youth know what we think of them, their behavior, abilities, and performance.

Direct feedback is the written or oral statements addressed to youth by significant adults and peers that evaluate, praise, reprimand, or criticize the youth's behavior, abilities, and performance. One example is the parent described above who yelled at his child, "You are so stupid!" Positive messages might be: "You are so smart. I knew you could do it," or "You are such a good helper. Thank you for putting away the dishes." The message might be delivered in a note put in the child's lunchbox that says, "You are special, and I love you."

Indirect feedback is the behaviors and communications, verbal and non-verbal, that adults and peers send indirectly regarding the youth's traits and competencies. A child's self-concept improves when adults listen to him and value his opinions. Warm hugs and celebrations of her efforts and successes let the child know that she is valued and you appreciate her hard work. A child's self-concept is threatened when they are ignored, never chosen to be on a team, or never have a parent attend their school events. The words are not spoken, but these indirect messages to the child about his importance, competency, and value are clear.

Task feedback is the results of one's efforts on different tasks, such as the completion of a project, accomplishment of a goal, or the winning of a competition. The reactions of significant people in the child's life can influence task feedback. If his accomplishments are ignored or put down as insignificant or negatively compared to others, the youth may believe that he is not, and can never be, good enough. To improve a child's self-concept, adults and peers need to acknowledge and praise his hard work and achievements.

Internalized feedback is the process whereby a person examines and evaluates his own abilities and behaviors. Adults need to point out to youth that their achievements and failures are a direct result of the youth's decisions, skills, and effort. If your mentee fails a test, help her examine and reflect on her own behavior—did she read the textbook; did she do all the homework; did she take and study class notes; did she review for the test? Ask her to plan what she can do differently to ensure that she passes the next test. If your mentee gets an "A" on her book report, ask her to read the teacher's comments or explain to you why she thought the teacher gave her a good grade.

If a child believes he is a failure, regardless of his abilities, he is more likely to make poor academic and social choices. If a child believes in his abilities to attain goals, he will achieve more and make choices that lead to life success.

Social, Academic, Physical, and Cultural Self-Concept

A person's self-concept can be divided into four major categories: social, academic, physical, and cultural. If a child has a positive self-concept in these four areas, she will have a strong sense of her own power, purpose, worth, and promise. However, young people can have a positive self-concept in one or more areas and a negative self-concept in others. For example, there are youth who will have a good social self-concept and a poor academic self-concept. They will function well in social settings and be well liked and accepted by their peers, yet struggle with beliefs that they are not intelligent and believe they are incapable of doing well in school. As a mentor, you will need to help your mentee develop a positive self-concept in all four areas.

Social Self-Concept refers to a youth's feelings and beliefs about his ability to interact with others in different social settings. Social self-concept is formed by the messages people receive about their social skills, appropriateness of their behavior, and the desirability of their presence in different environments. A positive social self-concept is important in providing teens with the confidence they need to make friends, participate in class and extra-curricular activities, interview for jobs and scholarships, and to work cooperatively with others.

Academic Self-Concept refers to a person's belief about his ability to learn and perform in an educational setting. Academic self-concept is formed by the messages a person receives from significant adults that tell them they are "stupid," "lazy," "dumb," "too slow," or that they are "smart," "intelligent," "hardworking," "good students." Children who do not believe they can do school assignments will find reasons not to do the work. They won't study or do their homework, they'll cut class, cheat, get sick so they can stay home, or they'll misbehave in class so they'll get kicked out.

Physical Self-Concept refers to a person's beliefs about their physical attractiveness and athletic abilities. Youth today are confronted with visual images in magazines, television, and movies about how an 'attractive' person should look. These illusions have led to eating disorders, use of diet pills and steroids, and obsessions with clothes and appearance.

Even though the parents, or you as the mentor, believe that the youth is just the right weight and is an attractive person without all the make-up, the adolescent will believe the messages sent to her by the media and her peers over anything adults may say. As teens struggle to adapt to their bodies' physical changes and work at being accepted by their peer group, their physical appearance often becomes more important to them than their education.

Cultural Self-Concept refers to what a person believes about himself as a member of a certain cultural group as a result of the messages he receives from significant others about the group's potential and value. The acceptance of societal stereotypes and prejudices regarding the youth's cultural group may create a negative cultural self-concept. A junior high teacher asked his Hispanic students why they didn't work harder in school, and one of the boys replied, "What do you expect? We're just 'dumb Mexicans.'" If your mentee is female, African American, obese, physically disabled, and from a low-income family, she belongs to five cultural groups that may be negatively labeled by society.

As a mentor, you need to be aware of and openly challenge the negative messages your mentee may be receiving about her cultural groups. Even if the messages are not directed specifically to your mentee, stereotypes and discriminatory behaviors about her cultural group will be internalized as personal assaults against her self-concept.

Indicators of a Positive Self-Concept

The *Positive Self-Concept Checklist* provides you with behavioral indicators of a person who has a positive social, academic, physical, and cultural self-concept. This checklist can be used to help you determine improvements in your mentee's self-concept as you do together some of the activities in the Building Self-Concept section of this unit.

Positive Self-Concept Checklist

Social Self-Concept

1. Participates in and enjoys group activities. _____
2. Treats people with respect and courtesy. _____
3. Exhibits good sportsmanlike behavior. _____
4. Is comfortable and confident interacting with others. _____
5. Is tolerant and accepting of human differences. _____
6. Is open to trying new experiences. _____
7. Says "no" to negative peer pressure. _____

Academic Self-Concept

1. Works to complete school assignments. _____
2. Has good school attendance. _____
3. Pays attention and participates in class. _____
4. Likes school. _____
5. Has good school behavior. _____
6. Enjoys learning new things. _____
7. Has short and long term educational and career goals. _____

Physical Self-Concept

1. Accepts compliments about appearance graciously. _____
2. Practices good hygiene. _____
3. Dresses appropriately for the occasion. _____
4. Sits and stands with good posture. _____
5. Has a healthy lifestyle. _____
6. Seeks professional medical help when needed. _____

Cultural Self-Concept

1. Expresses pride in his cultural group. _____
2. Participates in the activities of her cultural group. _____
3. Invites others to attend cultural group events. _____
4. Treats other cultural group members with respect. _____
5. Challenges stereotyped comments about his cultural group. _____

B. ADULT MESSAGES THAT IMPACT SELF-CONCEPT DEVELOPMENT

The development of a child's self-concept begins in the womb. Is the baby a welcome addition to the family or has an attempt been made to abort the child? Is there violence or harmony in the home? Does the mother take good care of her physical needs during pregnancy or does she smoke, drink, or use illegal drugs? These are indirect messages to the child about his self-worth, absorbed into his unconscious mind at a pre-linguistic level. The child does not have the words to express his sense of being welcomed or being unwanted, but the feelings will be there.

Once the child is born, adults continually send her messages about her self-worth. For a child to grow into a self-confident, empowered, happy adult, her caretakers need to provide her with all the components that go into developing a strong, positive self-concept.

Unconditional Love: The core of a child's self-concept is formed by receiving unconditional love from significant people in his life. Unconditional love means that someone accepts, values, and cares about him just as he is. Sometimes they may disapprove of the child's behavior, but the love and support is always there and communicated through direct and indirect messages.

Trust: The development of a healthy self-concept requires that a child learns to trust that his caretakers will meet his basic human needs for nutrition, rest, warmth, safety, and love. Scott Larson in *At Risk: Bringing Hope to Hurting Teenagers* states:

> "Unless the issue of trust is resolved for youth, they will remain stunted in their emotional and spiritual development. Honesty, consistency, and being a stable presence through both good and bad times are what lay the critical foundation of trust."

Positive Mirroring: Through eye contact, facial expressions, tone of voice, and touch, adults send messages to a child about her self-worth. The words "I love you" delivered in an angry voice, accompanied by a slap across the face, does not send the message that the adult really cares about the child and her feelings. A child can sense immediately, by watching adult body language, when she is welcomed and valued. When a child looks into the adult's face, she needs to see mirrored back to her in the adult's pleasant smile, friendly eyes, and gentle tone that she is safe and appreciated.

Belonging: Abraham Maslow identified levels of basic human needs that include a sense of belonging to a group. The need to belong to a group is very strong in adolescents. If a youth is not strongly bonded to his family, he will become overly attached to peer groups to fulfill his need to belong. Belonging to a group provides a sense of security and safety, and the group's cultural norms and rules provide structure and guidelines for living.

Being Needed: A child's self-concept will strengthen when she realizes that she is needed and has important contributions she can make to help others. When a child is given age-appropriate responsibilities, positive attention, and recognition for her contributions to the family and community, she will feel important and valued.

Positive Reinforcement: Children need positive reinforcement in the form of encouraging words and an occasional helping hand to keep them motivated and working towards their goals, especially when the going gets tough. When a youth becomes frustrated and wants to give up, someone needs to be there by his side with positive reinforcement. The adult does not do the work for him, but assists him in learning how to do the task and structuring the task into smaller components that can be successfully completed.

Positive and Negative Adult Messages

As a mentor, you will need to be careful that you do not send messages that may damage your mentee's self-concept. The following examples of adult behaviors that influence self-concept development provide you with ideas as to what adults do, consciously or unconsciously, that lead to positive and negative self-concepts in youth.

Adult Behaviors that Contribute to a Child's Negative Self-Concept:
- Ignoring the child and his needs.
- Comparing the child to other children.
- Labeling the child with nasty names.
- Abusing the child verbally, physically, or through neglect of his basic needs.
- Having age-inappropriate or unrealistic expectations and demands of the child.
- Having low expectations of the child, not expecting or asking her to perform up to her ability level.
- Publicly disciplining the child.

Adult Behaviors that Contribute to a Child's Positive Self-Concept:
- Spending quality time with the child.
- Listening to and valuing what the child says.
- Helping the child turn mistakes into learning experiences.
- Giving the child opportunities to learn and practice new skills.
- Attending his school and club events.
- Disciplining the child with respect, targeting only her behavior and not her as a person.
- Telling the child often that you care about him and think he is special.

Effects of Stereotypes & Discrimination on Self-Concept

Your mentee will be spending more time at school and out in the community than she will be with her own family and with you, her mentor. Be aware of the false messages she is given through others' stereotyped judgments and discriminatory behavior that negatively influence her self-concept.

A woman, who was a professional educator and whose Mexican husband was a lawyer, was approached by her daughter two weeks before she was to begin 8th grade. Her daughter was in tears and said she did not want to go back to school. She also said that she hated being Mexican. The teenager said that everyone in her school thought that Mexicans were all "fighters, alcoholics, and druggies," and she did not want to go back. The mother told her daughter that these were stereotypes and pointed out the many Hispanics in her life that were outstanding achievers and citizens. Her daughter replied, "Yes, I know that, but no one else in that school does. And they don't teach anything that talks about the good Hispanics." Her daughter went on to say that the girls in the cafeteria, making their weekend plans, would turn to her and say, "But you can't come, because you're a Mexican."

When you are with your mentee, look for the negative messages and discriminatory behaviors that affect her cultural group(s). For example:

- T-shirts and posters that put down women, gays or ethnic minority members.
- Buildings and playgrounds that are not handicap accessible.
- Songs on the radio that use swear words and derogatory names.
- Movies that portray certain cultural groups in a negative light without providing the balance of positive depictions of the cultural group.
- School and city programming that does not include important events for their cultural groups.
- Unequal treatment by police based on ethnicity and skin color.
- Lack of representation of her cultural group in government and school staffs.

Teens do not always feel comfortable talking about these injustices with their parents or friends. If you bring up the topic of prejudice and discrimination when encountered during your activities together, the youth may realize that you are someone he can talk to about the stereotyped put-downs and perceived discrimination he faces in school and in the community. Share with him similar incidents you have experienced and tell him how you did not let the prejudices of others interfere with your life success.

When your mentee uses language that is derogatory towards other groups or discriminates against others, point out to her the harm that such behavior does. Encourage her to be respectful of all cultural groups, as she would want others to respect her.

Culture Shock

Culture shock is an emotional and physical reaction brought about by immersion in a new and different culture. If your mentee is new to the school or community, especially if she is from a different country, she may experience culture shock. Everyone knows it is difficult to be the "new kid" in school. You have no friends or support system; you don't know the rules and routines; you may not understand English very well; you don't know who to ask for help; and you feel alone and isolated. The stress will affect the youth's schoolwork and may become so uncomfortable that he will skip class or drop out of school. His inability to function well in the new environment may also have a negative effect on his self-concept.

Symptoms of culture shock are similar to those of students identified as at-risk in our schools:

- Feelings of helplessness which may result in withdrawal and loneliness
- Irritability, anger, aggression
- Glazed staring
- Desire for home and the familiar
- Frustration, anxiety, paranoia
- Physical stress reactions such as headaches, nausea, fatigue, sleep disorders

The mentor can provide strong and vital support as her mentee works through her cultural shock and becomes competent in her new environment.

- Be sure she is given a tour of her new school and community.
- Introduce him to people who will be willing to assist and answer his questions.
- Explain that the feelings she may experience are a normal part of the adjustment process.
- Contact your mentee every day to discuss his concerns, answer questions, and encourage him to hang in there. Remind him that it takes time to adjust to a new setting, but you are confident that he will do fine.
- Discuss with your mentee's family that she may need more rest during the adjustment process, as the overload of new stimuli on her system can be very tiring.
- Provide your mentee with respite from the stress by taking him to lunch or a movie.
- Send lots of positive messages to your mentee that she is doing a good job and that you are proud of her efforts.

C. BUILDING SELF-CONCEPT

Focus on the Positive

I consulted with an elementary school in a low-income, Hispanic neighborhood where staff morale was low and student detentions and suspensions for misbehavior were high. The teachers were dreading going to work each day. Using a small amount of grant money, I suggested that we try to switch the focus to the students' positive behaviors. Together we developed PAL—Positive Action Lottery program. Staff gave students a ticket whenever they "caught" them doing something good. Good behavior could be working quietly at your desk, picking up trash from the floor, being nice to another student, and so forth. The students wrote their names on the tickets and put them in the lottery box. Every Friday the principal drew a primary and an intermediate student's name. These students were given a prize of school supplies, a game, or a book, and the principal sent letters to the parents letting them know their children were this week's PAL winners. The better students behaved, the more tickets they were given, which increased their chances of winning. Within one grading period, detentions and suspensions decreased 50%, teacher morale rose considerably, and everyone was enjoying going to school.

If children do not get enough adult attention through their positive behaviors, they will switch to negative acting-out. When you pay more attention to a youth's negative behavior, the misbehavior is reinforced and results in a continuation and increase of his misconduct. Then the adult gets more frustrated and angrier with the youth and may send messages directly and through their body language that the youth is unworthy and difficult to be around. As a mentor, be careful to keep your focus on your mentee's positive behaviors.

Accentuate the Positive

To increase your mentee's self-concept, look for and reinforce through praise, encouragement, and recognition, your mentee's positive behaviors.

- Wow! You didn't miss any school this grading period. Good for you.
- Thank you for letting me know you'd be late. That was very considerate of you, and I appreciate it.
- I enjoyed your program. I could tell you all worked hard to put the program together. You did a great job!
- You only missed three words on your spelling test. That's a big improvement over last week's test. Good work. Can I help you study for next week's test?

As the song goes—"accentuate the positive" and you'll help "eliminate the negative."

31

Praise and Encouragement

When your mentee does something well, has made improvements, or is trying really hard, you need to give her direct verbal *praise*.

- I knew you could!
- Fantastic! Excellent! Terrific!
- I'm proud of you.
- You're doing a good job.
- Now you have the hang of it.
- You outdid yourself today!
- You're getting better every day.

When your mentee gets frustrated or discouraged and wants to quit, you need to provide him words of *encouragement*.

- Keep it up!
- You can do it!
- Keep working on it; you're getting better.
- One more time and you'll have it.
- You never know until you try.

Your direct messages need to be delivered with body language and voice inflection that emphasizes your sincerity and confidence in his ability. Keep your praise genuine. Your mentee needs to be able to trust that you will be honest with him. Reinforce your words with gestures, such as giving her a "thumbs up" or a "high five," or a "yes" nod and a smile.

Follow your words of praise and encouragement with a description of the specific behavior you approve of and how the behavior benefits the youth and others. Occasionally, provide a reward that is meaningful to your mentee.

- All the studying you did for your math test paid off! You got a "B." You will need good math skills if you want to go into business.
- Your teacher said that she gave you the Excellent Citizen Award because you are always helpful in class, abide by the school rules, and volunteer to help with special needs students. This award will be a good addition to your college and scholarship applications.
- You have worked so hard on this social studies report. I know you will get a good grade. I think your hard work deserves a special treat; let's get some ice cream.

Reframing

By listening closely to your mentee's description of herself, you will be given clues to her self-concept. Her internal self-talk is continually repeating the perceived messages she has received from significant people in her life about her self-worth and ability.

- "I can't do anything right!"
- "I'm too stupid to go to college."
- "No way can I do this work. I give up!"
- "My parents don't care about me."

These words are a reflection of what he believes to be true about himself and lead to feelings of frustration, discouragement, despair, and anger. Because his self-talk is continually reminding him that he can't do it and no one really cares anyway, the youth may give up trying. He will not study; he'll ditch class; he'll blow-off the test. When the youth tells himself over and over that he is not capable of doing something, the words wear a path in his brain like a deep rut in the road that is difficult to move out of. He'll need your help.

When you hear your mentee saying negative things about her ability or worth, reframe what she has said into a more positive statement.

- Turn "I can't do anything right!" into *"There are lots of things you do very well. You're just having trouble doing this task. Let me help you get started."*
- Change "I'm too stupid to go to college" into *"I'm not sure who told you that, but I think you can get into college and graduate. It will take work, but you can do it."*
- Reword "No way I can do this homework. I give up!" to *"You sound overwhelmed. Let's see if we can break this problem down into smaller, more doable pieces. I know you'll be able to get it done then. Just hang in there. I'll help you."*
- Reframe "My parents don't care about me" to *"What makes you think that? I see a lot of ways they show you that they care."* Then mention a few ways.

Positive Affirmations

For those negative internal messages that seem resistant to change, ask your mentee if she would like to help her brain move down a different path. Use this manual to help explain to her how self-concept is developed and let her know she can change the negative messages to positive ones. Ask her what she would like to believe about herself. Help her form these beliefs into affirmation statements.

- I am an attractive person.
- I am smart.

- I'm good at learning new things.
- I am a good person.

Have her write down her affirmations 15 to 20 times, every day for a month. Have her say them to herself throughout the day. Have her write the affirmations on note cards and place them where she will see them to remind her to repeat them often. Explain that at first the message will seem strange and her brain will want to reject it. However, gradually, the new positive message will become more acceptable and will replace the negative, false belief. When her beliefs about herself become more positive, your mentee's self-concept will improve.

Success Journal

Buy your mentee a spiral notebook to use as his Success Journal. On the first few pages, ask him to make lists with the following headings:

- Things I Do Really Well
- Things I Have Done That I'm Proud Of
- What I Like About Myself.

Have him list at least 10 items under each heading. You might need to give him some examples to get him started.

- I'm good at math.
- I'm a good skateboarder.
- I work part-time after school and save my money.
- I help my sister with her homework.
- I'm a good listener.
- I care about my friends.

On the remaining notebook pages, ask your mentee to put the date and write down something he did successfully each day.

- I finished and turned in all my homework today.
- I carried the groceries from the car into the house for my mother.
- I let my little brother play with my Game Boy tonight.

Review the success journal each week with your mentee. When he starts to feel down on himself, suggest that he read through his success journal to remind him of the positive things he does and what a good person he is.

Activities that Improve Self-Concept

We know that a youth's self-concept is what she believes about herself based on what she thinks other people believe to be true about her. We learned that a youth's self-concept develops and changes over time based on the direct and indirect feedback she receives from significant people in her life. Self-concept building activities are designed to give your mentee positive feedback messages about her behavior, abilities, and performance. These activities provide your mentee with opportunities to demonstrate his abilities, learn and practice new skills, and to help others. Be sure to give your mentee direct positive messages about his performance during and after these activities; reinforce the positive feedback he will receive from others.

Social Self-Concept

- Find out what special interests or talents your mentee has and incorporate these interests into your activities together; i.e., bowling, karaoke, fishing, gardening, making pottery.
- Teach and practice new social skills by attending a play or going to a restaurant where you are seated by the hostess and order from a menu.
- Create opportunities to develop relationship skills by partnering with other mentors and their mentees to play games, make crafts, etc.
- Do community volunteer work together. Check the newspaper or call United Way to learn about volunteer opportunities.
- Spend time actively listening to what your mentee has done during the week. Ask for details; let her know that you are truly interested.

Academic Self-Concept

- Play problem-solving games together; i.e., checkers, Chinese checkers, chess, Scrabble, Charades, puzzles.
- Attend your mentee's school programs and provide her with specific feedback about what you liked.
- Ask to read your mentee's school papers, reports, and essays and give him both positive and constructive feedback about his work.
- Help your mentee learn from her mistakes by discussing what she could do differently to improve her work.
- Have mini-celebrations when he works hard and makes improvements in his schoolwork.

Physical Self-Concept

- Shop for and prepare healthy meals together.
- Take salsa or swing dance lessons.
- Take your female mentees for the free makeovers provided by department and bath product stores. Be sure to get the parents approval for this activity.

- Develop a healthy habits plan and agree to both stick to the plan for at least one week.
- Do aerobic activities such as roller skating, hiking, swimming, or biking.

Cultural Self-Concept

- Attend cultural events such as Cinco de Mayo and Juneteenth celebrations, Cherry Blossom Festival, or a Native American Pow Wow.
- Check out and watch videos from the library on her cultural heritage.
- Read books or poetry by authors from his cultural group
- Take trips to cultural museums and art galleries.

Explore with your mentee the activities that are available in your community. Take turns deciding what you will do each week, and make a commitment to stay open to trying new things.

Remembrance Album

Another strategy for nurturing your mentee's self-concept is to develop positive memories. Purchase or make a scrapbook for your mentee where you both can put mementos of your time together; i.e., ticket stubs, matchbook covers, concert programs, a leaf collected during a hike, and so forth. Take photos during your activities. Write down special tidbit memories. Include the dates and locations of each event. Share the scrapbook with your mentee's family. The remembrance album will make your mentee feel very special and provide her with a lasting, positive memory of your mentoring relationship.

UNIT TWO: BIBLIOGRAPHY

Brendtro, Brokenleg and Bockern. (1990). *Reclaiming Youth At Risk: Our Hope for the Future.* Bloomington, IN: National Educational Service.

Burke, Raymond V. (1996). *Common Sense Parenting.* Boys Town, NE: Boys Town Press.

Byrne, B. (1990). "Self-concept and academic achievement: Investigating their importance as discriminators of academic track membership in high school." *Canadian Journal of Education, 15(2),* 173-182.

Child Development Network. (2003). *Self Concept and Self Esteem.* http://www.child-developmentnet.com/clinical/general/selfconcept.html. (accessed on 5/27/05)

El Paso County Family Preservation Program. "97 Ways to Say 'Very Good'." Colorado Springs, CO: Chins Up Youth and Family Services.

Gabelko and Michaelis. (1981). *Reducing Adolescent Prejudice: A Handbook.* New York, NY: Teachers College, Columbia University.

Gordon, Jan. Ohio State University Fact Sheet. *Building Children's Self-esteem.* http://ohioline.osu.edu/hyg-fact/5000/5263.html. (accessed on 5/27/05)

Gwynne, Robert. (1997). *Maslow's Hierarchy of Needs.* http://www.utk.edu/?gwynne/ maslow.htp (accessed 6/10/05)

Heacox, Diane. (1991). *Up From Underachievement: How Teachers, Students, and Parents Can Work Together to Promote Student Success."* Minneapolis, MN: Free Spirit Publishing.

Healthy Communities, Healthy Youth. (2004) "40 Developmental Assets." Minneapolis, MN: Search Institute. http://www.search-institute.org/assets/assetcategories.html. (accessed on 5/20/05).

Huitt,W. (2004). Self-concept and Self-esteem. *Educational Psychology Interactive.* Valdosta, GA: Valdosta State University. http://chiron.valdosta.edu/whuitt/col/regsys/self.html. (accessed 5/27/05)

Kuykendall, Crystal. (1992). *From Rage to Hope: Strategies for Reclaiming Black & Hispanic Students.* Bloomington, IN: National Educational Service.

Larson, Scott. (1999). *At Risk: Bringing Hope to Hurting Teenagers.* Loveland, CO: Group Publishing.

Luna, F.C. and Miller, Carol L. (2002). *Closing the Achievement Gap.* Ft. Collins, CO: Rocky Mountain Intercultural Institute.

Mercer, Johnny and Arlen, Harold. (1944). *Accentuate the Positive.*

Miller, Carol L. and VanDecar, Elena. (2004). *Parenting for Academic Success.* Denver, CO: Latin American Research and Service Agency.

Roehlkepartain, Jolene L. "150 Ways to Show Kids You Care." Minneapolis, MN: Search Institute. www.search-institute.org. (accessed 5/20/05)

Scholl, Beauvais, and Leonard. (2002). *Self Concept Based Motivation.* http://www.cba.rui.edu/School/Notes/Self_Concept_Model.html. (accessed on 5/27/05)

Scriptographic Booklet. (1987). *Let's Learn About Self-Esteem.* South Deerfield, MA: Channing L. Bete Co. Inc.

UNIT THREE: COMMUNICATION SKILLS

A. **Unit Introduction**

   What Are Communication Skills?
   Why Are Communication Skills Important?
   Communication Skills: Need for Improvement Checklist

B. **Listening Skills**

   Are You A Good Listener?
   Tips for Listening
   Get the Entire Message
   Activities to Practice Listening Skills

C. **Speaking Skills**

   Mentoring Techniques for Developing Speaking Skills
   Using Effective Speaking Skills
   Ineffective Messages: Communication Barriers
   Activities to Practice Speaking Skills

D. **Reading for Everyday Living**

   Reading for Everyday Living Activities
   Reading for Moral and Social Development
   Analyzing Books for Bias
   Multicultural Books for Teens and Young Adults

E. **Writing for Everyday Living**

   Writing for Everyday Living Activities

A. WHAT ARE COMMUNICATION SKILLS

Communication is the exchange of ideas, information, and meaning through listening and reading, speaking and writing, non-verbal body language, and voice inflection. Communication requires at least two people—the sender and the receiver of the message. In their book *The Successful Child*, Sears and Sears explain:

"Good communication is knowing when to speak and when to keep silent. It's being able to understand what your words may mean to another person, and to be a good listener. Being able to communicate well is related to other qualities associated with kids who turn out well: self-esteem, empathy, sensitivity, kindness."

In Unit Three, we will learn about communication skills used in everyday living.

Why Are Communication Skills Important?

Most aspects of successful living require good communication skills.

- Sara boarded the wrong bus and is lost. She needs *to ask for and follow directions.*
- Jose helped Sara find her way home because he could *give good directions.*
- Donna passed her driving test because she *read and studied the manual.*
- Matt got the job at the drive-in because he *filled out the application and had a good job interview.*
- Tomas *negotiated* a later curfew with his father for prom night
- When Angie was angry with her little brother, she was able to *express her feelings in an appropriate way.*
- In the *letter she wrote* to her grandmother, LeXuan *shared her camping experience.*

Mentors need to help their mentees learn and practice communication skills. Use the *Communication Skills: Need for Improvement Checklist* to determine some of the communication areas your mentee may need to change and improve.

Communication Skills: Need for Improvement Checklist

Listening
- Interrupts when others are talking.
- Is easily distracted; mind seems to wander when others are talking.
- Does not look at the person who is talking.
- Responds inappropriately to what others are saying.
- Does not show respect to the speaker.

Speaking
- Does not speak English well.
- Has a limited vocabulary.
- Has poor telephone etiquette.
- Uses a lot of slang and uh's when speaking.
- Finishes sentences for the person speaking.

Reading
- Can't read and follow basic directions.
- Has never read a book without pictures in her leisure time.
- Does not have a public library card.
- Does not know how to use the Internet to obtain basic information.

Writing
- Has sloppy handwriting; others can't read his handwriting.
- Doesn't know how to fill out basic forms.
- Doesn't know how to write a formal letter or address an envelope.

Body Language
- Rarely looks at you when speaking.
- Slouches, hangs her head down, or folds her arms.
- Taps foot repetitively; fidgets; squirms.
- Glares and frowns a lot for no apparent reason.

Use of Voice
- Speaks too softly for you to hear or speaks too loudly for the occasion.
- Speaks in a monotone, with no enthusiasm.
- Speaks too fast, slurring words together into one long word.

B. LISTENING SKILLS

Have any of the following scenarios happened to you?

- While you're trying to discuss a project with your supervisor or teacher, she is answering the phone, reading her email, opening her snail mail, and letting other people come into the office.
- Someone asks you a question, and then he interrupts you while you are answering and changes the subject.
- You are giving someone directions, and she walks away when you are in mid-sentence.
- Sometimes you feel like yelling, "You're not listening to me!"

A common complaint of adolescents is that adults do not listen to them, and adults who work with teenagers will sometimes tell them, "You're not hearing me. Read my lips! What did I just say?"

Find out how you and your mentee rate as listeners by taking the *Are You A Good Listener* survey together. Discuss your answers and then go over the *Tips for Listening* to find out what you can do to improve your listening skills.

Are You a Good Listener?

	Always	Sometimes	Never
1. Do you listen even if you don't like the person speaking?			
2. Do you listen equally well whether the person is male, female, young, or old?			
3. Do you listen to others without interrupting them before they have finished speaking?			
3. Do you think about what is being said?			
4. Do you ignore or try to minimize the distractions around you?			
5. Do you try to understand what the message is beyond the actual words being spoken?			
6. Do you restate an idea and ask if you have understood correctly?			
7. Do you withhold judgment on an idea until you have heard all of it?			
8. Do you listen regardless of the manner of speaking and choice of words?			
9. Do you ask for clarification of words and terms you don't understand?			
10. Do you ask questions in order to have an idea explained more fully?			
11. Do you continue listening when you disagree with the speaker?			
12. Do you give your full attention to the person speaking, never trying to accomplish other tasks as you listen?			
13. Do you look at the person who is talking, showing by your facial expressions that you are listening?			

Tips for Listening

1. **Get Rid of Distractions.** Put down whatever you have in your hands. Turn off the CD player or television. Find a quiet place where you can talk without interruptions.

2. **Stop Talking.** You cannot listen if you are talking. A good listener waits patiently until the other person is finished speaking and does not interrupt with questions or comments.

3. **Act Like You're Interested.** Be alert. Let your face and body language reflect your interest in what the speaker is saying.

4. **Look at the Other Person.** The speaker's body language is usually more important than the actual words. You cannot observe facial expressions, hand movements, and body posture if you are not looking at the speaker.

5. **Get the Main Idea.** Try to listen for the important points the speaker is trying to make.

6. **Ask Questions:** When you don't understand, need further clarification, or want to demonstrate that you are listening, ask appropriate questions.

7. **Check for Understanding:** To be sure you understand what is being said, rephrase what you think the speaker is saying, and ask, "Is this what you mean? Am I understanding you correctly?"

8. **React to Ideas, Not to the Person.** Don't let your feelings about the speaker influence how you interpret his words. Good ideas can come from people whose looks or personality you don't like.

9. **Avoid Hasty Judgments. Don't Argue Mentally.** Wait until all the facts are in before making any judgments about what the speaker is saying. Don't be forming argumentative responses in your mind while you are listening.

10. **Don't Antagonize the Speaker.** The speaker may shut down and quit talking if you do things that are annoying and disrespectful while they are speaking; i.e., yawning, staring at the clock, turning your back to them.

Get the Entire Message

Just listening to the words will not give you the entire message. Research tells us that most of what the speaker is trying to say is contained in his non-verbal behavior. Ask your mentee to imagine the following teenagers:

Person A: His arms are crossed; his foot is tapping; he is frowning.
Person B: She has a big smile; she looks relaxed.
Person C: His head is down; his shoulders are bent forward; he does not make eye contact.

Ask her what messages are being sent by the young people's body language.

Now picture each of these youth saying the words, "I'm fine." How does this verbal message change when you consider their body language? How will their words sound? When you and your mentee are out in public, make a game of watching people's body language and guessing how they might be feeling.

Activities to Practice Listening Skills

The Gossip Chain: With a group of other mentors and mentees, play the Gossip Chain. Sit in a circle. In a whisper, have one person make up a story or read a juicy letter from *Dear Abby* to the person next to him. That person repeats the story to the person next to her until the story is passed around the entire circle. The last person in the chain will say what she heard out loud for everyone to hear. This game demonstrates how a person only hears certain parts of the story and sometimes makes up information to fill-in what they missed.

For added fun, find two people who speak a different language. Ask the first bilingual person to translate the story from English into the second language. Then the second bilingual person translates the story back into English. This exercise shows you how much information can be lost or distorted during translation.

Simon Says: This game is not just for little kids. Teens and adults can have a lot of fun and sharpen their listening skills by playing Simon Says. Someone has to be Simon and give directions to the others. "Simon says to hop on your left foot." "Simon Says to turn around three times." If the person who is Simon begins with "Simon Says," everyone has to follow the directions. If the person playing the role of Simon does not begin with "Simon Says," you just stand still and do nothing. If the direction is "Hop on your left foot," and you hop on your left foot, then you become Simon because the directions did not begin with "Simon Says."

Pass It On: You can play Pass It On with a group or with just you and your mentee. Someone starts telling a story, gets to a critical point in the plot and then passes on to the next person who will continue the story. This game helps you practice listening and speaking skills. Tape record or videotape each storyteller to play back later—maybe at a holiday celebration when family members are present. Some story starters you can use are:

A. Tomorrow, I leave on the first manned shuttle to Mars.
B. My best friend, Jen, didn't make it home after the party.
C. The 5:00 news reported that a lion had escaped from the zoo.
D. My 16th birthday party was a disaster.

Movies, TV Shows, Books on Tape: Try some of the following activities to sharpen your mentee's listening skills.

* Turn the sound off when you watch television. Watch the actors' body language. See if you can tell what is going on without hearing the words.
* Play a DVD movie in another language. Can you tell what the plot is?
* Listen to books on cassettes or CDs while you're riding in the car, working on projects, or doing volunteer work together. See if you laugh in the same places or have the same reactions to what is happening. You can check audio books out for free from the library.
* Discuss movies that you watch together. Share what you each thought about the storyline and characters. How would you rate the movie on a scale of 1 to 10? Were there any stereotypes or other offensive portrayals in the movie? What would you tell other people about the movie?

Listening to Directions: Find a recipe you both want to try. You read the directions while your mentee listens and follows them. Be sure to watch closely in case she puts in baking soda instead of baking powder.

Tape-recorded Tours: Art Galleries, zoos, national parks, and museums now have tape-recorded tours that explain what you are seeing. Take one of these tours. See what you both learn.

Trust Walks: You do this activity with a partner. One person is blindfolded, and the other person gives oral directions. The goal is to go from Point A to Point B through an obstacle course. The course could be a playground, nature hike, or someone's backyard, using chairs, ladders, balls, and other household items. The person giving the directions has to be precise, and the blindfolded person has to listen closely. To make it a competition when others play with you, time how long it takes people to complete the course. The team with the fastest time is the winner.

C. SPEAKING SKILLS

One of the scariest subjects in school for many high school students is the required speech class. Standing in front of a group and talking is a challenge even for some adults. People get flustered, have trouble breathing, forget what they were going to say, and stumble over their words. Yet being able to express yourself and share what you know with others is critical to life success. Consider the following situations where good speaking skills are important:

- Participating in class discussions
- Answering teachers' questions
- Interviewing for a job
- Giving presentations at work
- Training a new employee
- Networking with potential customers and colleagues
- Explaining to the doctor how you feel
- Talking with your child's teacher about your concerns
- Calling the police for assistance
- Teaching your child safety rules

Your mentee may have good conversational skills in casual or informal English but have limited formal or academic English ability. In her book, *A Framework for Understanding Poverty*, Ruby Payne explains:

" . . . to get a well-paying job, it is expected that one will be able to use formal register (English). Ability to use formal register is a hidden rule of the middle class. The inability to use it will knock one out of an interview in two or three minutes. The use of formal register, on the other hand, allows one to score well on tests and do well in school and higher education."

Your mentee may be an ELL (English Language Learner) student who is learning English as her second language. Whether your mentee is an ELL student or only speaks informal, casual English, she will need your assistance in learning to speak formal English and opportunities to practice speaking in real life situations. Read over the following *Mentoring Techniques for Developing Speaking Skills*. These techniques will guide you as you provide your mentee with the support she needs in learning how to speak formal English.

Mentoring Techniques for Developing Speaking Skills

1. Be a good model of language skills by speaking formal English clearly, using words that can be understood.

2. Do not put down or discount the language your mentee's family speaks. Explain that everyone uses what is called "code switching" where they change their speech patterns to speak in a manner that is appropriate and acceptable for different settings. For example, teenagers use the current slang words; coaches and sport's writers have a unique descriptive vocabulary; lawyers and judges speak in "legaleze."

3. When your mentee uses incorrect terms or grammar, repeat their words using the correct words and grammar. They may say, "This ain't for me." You respond, "This isn't for you? Why not?"

4. Find opportunities for your mentee to learn and practice his speaking abilities in different real-life settings.

5. Praise and encourage your mentee's progress in learning and speaking formal English.

6. Develop a trust relationship that allows your mentee to ask questions about the correct words and grammar to use without feeling embarrassed or ashamed.

7. Be patient and give your mentee "wait time" to formulate his thoughts and figure out what he wants to say. ELL students may be translating English into their home language, deciding what they want to say, and then translating their words back into English before they verbally respond to your questions.

8. Use open-ended questions that require your mentee to respond with more than a "yes" or "no" answer.

9. Help your mentee understand the importance of formal English speaking abilities in doing well in school, getting and keeping a job, and being an active member of one's community.

Using Effective Speaking Skills

Communication styles are culturally laden. Your mentee may come from a country where eye contact, male-female role behaviors, and verbal directness may differ from expectations in the United States. Explain again the importance of "code switching" and using the communication style that is appropriate for the setting and people you are addressing.

Non-assertive / Aggressive / Assertive Verbal Behaviors: A person's self-concept and attitude towards others are reflected in their communication style. Consider the following behavior comparisons:

Non-Assertive Verbal Behavior:

The person is apologetic, rambles, is disconnected, hesitant, and fails to express his ideas or wants.

Example: *I've got something to tell you . . . I mean . . . Do you want to hear it?*

Aggressive Verbal Behavior:

The person is angry, accusing, sarcastic, demanding, and uses 'you' messages that blame and label others.

Example: *Hey you! Shut up! Listen to me!*

Assertive Verbal Behavior:

The person is objective, direct, honest, reasonable, and uses 'I' messages.
Example: *I would like you to listen to what I have to say.*

Non-assertive people are hesitant to ask for what they need and want.
Aggressive people only upset others who then refuse to listen or help.
Assertive people ask calmly for what they want and have a much better chance of getting their needs met.

"I" Message: "I" messages convey the speaker's feelings and needs in a way that is more likely to get a positive response. An "I" message:

•   Describes a behavior without attacking the person.
•   Describes a specific incident rather than 'everything' and 'always'.
•   Expresses your feelings and reactions rather than placing blame.
•   Does not infer meaning to another's behavior.

Instead of: *I can't trust you! You are always late! You never think about what I need. You only care about yourself.*

An effective "I" message would be: *I was disappointed and frustrated when you were an hour late picking me up. I felt like you didn't care about my feelings. I would appreciate it if you would call me next time you think you'll be late.*

Asking for What You Need: Encourage your mentee to ask for what he needs, including requesting permission, asking for help, or telling you what he wants to do. A few pointers in making the ask are:

- Ask the person most likely to provide you with assistance.
- Look directly at the person you are asking.
- Be pleasant and polite.
- Be specific about your request so the other person knows exactly what you want.
- Ask instead of demand, saying, "Would you please... "
- Be clear about your reasons for asking.
- Accept the person's decision graciously.
- Thank the person.

Remind your mentee that we don't always get what we ask for; but if we don't ask, we will rarely get what we want.

Language Etiquette: I am always surprised at the number of youth and adults who do not have good language etiquette. Good conversation manners include:

- Using 'please' and 'thank you.'
- Introducing oneself and other people properly.
- Standing up when you are being introduced to people and politely saying that you are pleased to meet them.
- Answering the telephone correctly and taking phone messages.
- Using respectful terms like 'sir' and 'ma'am.'
- Addressing a person by Mr. or Ms. unless given permission to use their first names.
- Learning how to pronounce names correctly.
- Looking at the person to whom you are talking.

Model good language etiquette for your mentee. You may have to directly instruct or at times remind her to speak respectfully. Polite language makes a very good first impression and demonstrates to the other person that you are someone they would like to get to know better.

Body Language: As discussed in the Listening Skills section, your body language communicates the intent of your message more than your actual words. Remind your mentee to be aware of his facial expressions, posture, hand movements, and eye contact when he is speaking to others. A smile communicates friendliness and welcome. Good posture and direct eye contact communicate that he is self-confident and interested in the conversation. Speaking with enthusiasm and energy engages the listener.

Ineffective Messages: Communication Barriers

Often the messages we send block or interfere with communication in ways that are harmful to relationships and problem solving. Go over the following examples of ineffective messages with your mentee. Ask him how he would turn the messages into effective ones.

- Criticizing / Judging—*It's your own stupid fault.*
- Name-calling / Put-downs—*Hey punk! Get out of my face!*
- Diagnosing / Analyzing—*You're only doing that to annoy me.*
- Ordering / Demanding—*Do it now! Stop whining!*
- Threatening / Warning—*Do that again and I'll deck you!*
- Preaching—*You should have done what I told you to do.*
- Excessive questioning—*Why did you do that? What were you thinking?*
- Withdrawing—*Let's just forget it. I don't want to talk about it.*

Activities to Practice Speaking Skills

Vocabulary Builders: Help your mentee develop a vocabulary building system to record unfamiliar words and their definitions. A spiral notebook or 3" x 5" index cards kept in a file box and organized alphabetically work well. During activities or field trips or while watching movies or listening to the radio, have your mentee listen for words that are unfamiliar to her. Have her write the word in her notebook, look up the definition in the dictionary, and use the word in a sentence. You can model the value of vocabulary building by pointing out words you don't recognize and putting them in your own notebook.

Telephone Etiquette: Teach your mentee how to answer your phone politely and then ask him to practice by answering your phone when you are together. Be sure he introduces himself, explains that he is a friend of yours, and then asks politely what the caller wants. If you are busy, teach your mentee to record the caller's name, phone number, and time of the call. Ask him to assure the caller that he will pass on the message, thank them for calling, and then say good-bye politely.

Introductions: Many adolescents are reluctant and shy about introducing themselves. They will only give their first name, often said in a whisper while they are looking at the floor. Have your mentee practice saying, "Hello, my name is (first and last names); I'm pleased to meet you." While she is introducing herself, ask her to smile, look you in the eye, and extend her hand for a handshake. Then ask her to practice introducing you to other people, "This is my mentor (your first and last names)." When you meet new people, have your mentee practice making polite, assertive introductions.

Ordering Food: Have your mentee place phone orders for pizza or take-out food you will pick up on your way home. Or, have him do the ordering from a menu when you are eating at restaurants. Discuss conversation etiquette such as saying "please" and "thank you" and the importance of giving clear, easily understood directions. Have him practice "asking for what he needs" when his food is not prepared well or the order is incorrect.

Asking and Giving Directions: The games described in the Activities to Practice Listening Skills section can also be used in developing speaking skills. When your mentee is Simon, she must think up and give Simon Says directions. Have your mentee give you the recipe directions while you make cookies or dinner. Have her verbally guide you through the Trust Walk. Ask your mentee to be the caller for Bingo or Loteria (Mexican Bingo).

Tutoring Younger Children: Assist your mentee in helping a younger sibling or friend with schoolwork or reading books. You can model how to give oral directions and provide positive support, constructive feedback, and praise. As your mentee learns to use his language skills to help others, you can gradually take a smaller and smaller role in the process.

Field Trip Experiences: One goal of language learning is to be able to interact in the real world where language is used. Your mentee needs to observe and experience how people use academic English in the real world, outside of the classroom. Take him to museums, science exhibits, art galleries, the zoo, and tours of university campuses, military bases, hospitals, and manufacturing plants—places where he will be exposed to people speaking academic English. Encourage him to interact with tour guides, professors, doctors, college students, and business professionals. Discuss these experiences with your mentee and have him add new words he learned to his vocabulary building system. The new words will have more meaning now because your mentee can match the words with the experiences you provided him.

Sharing Experiences and Stories: During your time together, share with each other what has happened during the previous week. Encourage your mentee to talk with her family about the activities she does with you. Draw her into conversations. Listen attentively as she talks, and then ask questions that will encourage her to provide more information.

D. READING FOR EVERYDAY LIVING

Techniques for reading textbooks will be covered in the Study Skills Unit. In this section, the focus will be on reading skills needed for everyday living. People who are illiterate or who have limited reading ability have a difficult time accessing services, are limited in their job choices, and are unable to learn new information from books and the Internet. Good reading skills are required for:

- Reading directions
- Using maps
- Looking up numbers in a telephone book
- Reading the want-ads
- Ordering from a menu
- Filling out forms
- Taking the driver's license test
- Reading street signs
- Reading labels and advertisements
- Understanding contracts
- Helping your children with homework
- Reading notices from school and work
- Voting
- Reading magazines and books for entertainment
- Reading newspapers to be a well-informed citizen

When you are with your mentee, be aware of the *need to read.*

Reading for Everyday Living Activities

Find reading opportunities to do with your mentee. Below are some suggestions:

- Go to the library and look for magazines that would interest your mentee. Read them while you are at the library or check them out to read later. Be sure your mentee uses his own library card and knows when the magazines have to be returned. When you find out what magazines your mentee enjoys, consider purchasing him copies as a gift or reward for jobs well done.
- Check to see if your mentee knows how to access information from the Internet. If not, help him search different topics that interest him.
- Go for a soda or coffee and read the newspaper together. Discuss the news found in different sections of the paper: current events, community news, entertainment, sports, comics, want ads, etc.

- Teach your mentee how to use city maps and ask her to be the navigator when you are going to different locations.
- Ask your mentee to use the newspaper or the Internet to look up movie listings and start times.
- During elections, read the sample ballots together. Discuss the pros and cons of issues and candidates. Show him how to register to vote.
- Pick up a copy of the motor vehicle manual and help her study for the written part of her driver's test.
- Buy a new game and ask your mentee to read the directions while you both learn how to play.
- Share with your mentee how you use reading for your job.
- You and your mentee could join a book club or reading group in your community or on-line. Two websites to get you started are Book-Clubs-Resource.com or Face-to-Face and Virtual Book Clubs & Reading Groups at http://eduscapes. com/tap/topic112.htm.

Once you start paying attention to the "need to read," you will find lots of opportunities for your mentee to practice reading skills.

Reading for Moral and Social Development

Reading books can provide you and your mentee with a source of social action topics to discuss and ponder. The Council on Interracial Books for Children explains that children's books carry a moral message that molds young minds. In their *Guidelines for Selecting Bias-Free Textbooks and Storybooks*, they propose that "children's literature become a means for the conscious promotion of human values that will help lead to greater human liberation."

In our increasingly diverse nation, learning about and becoming comfortable with cultural differences will be important for your mentee. Many books reinforce stereotypes and perpetuate false ideas about people from different cultures. Read the *Analyzing Books for Bias* checklist and use these guidelines to help you and your mentee critique books you have read.

A list of books by well-known and respected authors from ethnic minority groups is provided at the end of this section. Another source of excellent multicultural books are those that have been given awards or are recommended by the following groups:

- *Asian Pacific American Award for Literature* (http://www.apalaweb.org/awards). Presented by the Asian/Pacific American Librarians Association to Asian Pacific American authors.
- *The Oyate Organization* (http://oyate.org). Oyate is a Native organization working

to see that the lives and histories of Native American people are portrayed honestly and with respect.

- *Pura Belpré Award* (http://www.acs.ucalgary.ca). Awarded every two years by the Association for Library Service to Children and the National Association to Promote Library Services to the Spanish-speaking to honor Latino writers and illustrators whose work best portrays and celebrates the Latino cultural experience in a work of literature for youth.

- *Américas Award* (http://www.uwm.edu/Dept/CLACS/outreach/americas.html). Awarded by the Consortium of Latin American Studies Programs to U.S. works of fiction, poetry, folklore or selected non-fiction published in English or Spanish that authentically and engagingly portray Latin America, the Caribbean, or Latinos in the United States.

- *Coretta Scott King Award* (http://www.acs.ucalgary.ca/~dkbrown/coretta.thml) Awarded by the American Library Association Social Responsibilities Round Table to an African American author and an African American illustrator for an outstandingly inspirational and educational contribution to children's literature.

- *Children's Book Committee at Bank Street College.* Awarded to works for children or young people that "deal realistically and in a positive way with problems in their world."

- *Jane Addams Book Award.* Awarded to the book that most effectively promotes the cause of peace, social justice, and world community.

Discussion Questions: Use some of the following questions in your discussions of books you and your mentee have read.

1. What did this book teach you?
2. How were the characters alike? Different?
3. Choose an incident where one of the characters had to make a decision. What would you have done?
4. Did you find any bias in the story? (See Analyzing Books for Bias.)
5. What moral value(s) is the author promoting in the story?
6. Which character could you relate to best and why?
7. What do you think will be your lasting impression of the book?
8. Would you recommend this book to a friend? Why or why not?

Analyzing Books for Bias*

I. Background of the Author

Read the brief author biography usually found at the beginning or end of the novel or on the inside cover. Is the author a member of the culture about which he is writing? Has he done research to ensure that his portrayal of the culture is accurate? Has the book been reviewed and endorsed by members of the culture?

2. Check the Story Line

Are mainstream cultural values being used as the standard for success? Are women and ethnic minorities in hero, villain, or victim roles? Who are the problem-solvers? Are real life issues addressed only from a dominant culture perspective?

3. Watch for Loaded Words

Are words with offensive and racist overtones used to describe characters, such as "savage, primitive, sinister, sly, cunning, lazy, backward, dumb?" Are male gender instead of gender-neutral terms used; i.e., fireman or firefighter; pioneer and his wife or the pioneers; policeman or police officer?

4. Check the Illustrations

Are people of color depicted as genuine individuals with distinctive features or do they "all look alike" and dress in stereotypical clothing. Are males the "doers" and females the "observers?" Is the full range of humanity depicted in scenes?

5. Consider the Effects on a Child's Self-Concept

Will reading the book make minority children feel that their language, viewpoints, and culture are inferior, or make dominant culture children feel they are superior? Are there characters in the story with whom a minority child can identify in a positive way?

6. Historical Accuracy / Cultural Authenticity

Are the contributions of minority groups and women to the life and culture of the United States fully included? Is history written from a Eurocentric, dominant culture perspective? Are minority cultures and customs distorted or trivialized?

*Adapted from *Guidelines for Selecting Bias-Free Textbooks and Storybooks.*

Multicultural Books for Teens and Young Adults

Middle School

The After Life by Gary Soto
Child Bride by Ching Yeung Russell
The Clay Marble by Minfong Ho
Close To the Heart by Diane Gonzales Bertrand
Fallen Angels by Walter Dean Myers
Gathering the Dew by Minfong Ho
The Girl on the Outside by Mildred Pitts Walter
Ghost Train by Papul Yee
The Hate Crime by Phyllis Karas
Heaven by Angela Johnson
Her Stories by Virginia Hamilton
Hoops by Walter Dean Myers
Journey Home by Yoshiko Uchida
Leon's Story by Leon Walter Tillage
Lorenzo's Revolutionary Quest by Lila and Rick Guzman
My Sister Annie by Bill Dodds
Navajo Code Talkers by Nathan Aaseng
Pacific Crossing by Gary Soto
Pocahontas by Joseph Bruchac
Rice Without Rain by Minfong Ho
Squanto's Journey by Joseph Bruchac
The Summer of Pintor by Ofelia Dumas Lachtman
Taking Sides by Gary Soto
Teen Angel by Gloria Velasquez
The Traitor by Laurence Yep
Trion's Choice by Diane Gonzales Bertran Guzman
Walking Star by Victor Villasenor
Water Ghost by Ching Yeung Russell
Which Way Freedom by Joyce Hansen
The Young Landlords by Walter Dean Myers

Multicultural Books for Teens and Young Adults

High School Books

145th Street: Short Stories by Walter Dean Myers
Across the Great River by Irene Beltran Hernandez
Bird Girl by Velma Wallis
Bless Me, Ultima by Rudolfa Anaya
The Bluest Eyes by Toni Morrison
Bronx Masquerade by Nikki Grimes
China Boy by Gus Lee
Dawn Land by Joseph Bruchac
Finding My Voice by Marie G. Lee
Greater Than Angels by Carol Matas
The House on Mango Street by Sandra Cisceros
How the Garcia Girls Lost Their Accents by Julia Alvarez
Interpreter of Maladies by Jhumpa Lahiri
Let The Circle Be Unbroken by Mildred D. Taylor
Like Sisters on the Homefront by Rita Williams-Garcia
Long River by Joseph Bruchac
MACHO! by Victor Villasenor
Maizon at Blue Hill by Jacqueline Woodson
Night Flying Woman: An Ojibway Narrative by Ignatia Broker
Plain City by Virginia Hamilton
The Road to Memphis by Mildred D. Taylor
Roll of Thunder, Hear My Cry by Mildred D. Taylor
Shifting Loyalties by Daniel Cano
So Far From God by Ana Castillo
To Be A Slave by Julius Lester
Two Old Women by Wilma Wallis
The Ways of My Grandmothers by Beverly Hungry Wolf

E. WRITING SKILLS FOR EVERYDAY LIVING

The ability to write is necessary for successful living in the 21st century. People who cannot read or write will find it difficult to function without assistance. As we did in Reading Skills for Everyday Living, consider the following list of tasks that require the ability to write:

- Filling out forms
- Writing checks or money orders
- Writing notes to your child's teacher
- Keeping a calendar of important dates and meetings
- Taking written tests for school, work, and licenses
- Writing reports for work or school
- Filling out job applications
- Writing letters or emails
- Addressing envelopes
- Making to-do lists

Writing is a skill that needs to be practiced. Some high school students have good conversational English skills but cannot write a simple sentence. They can tell you what they want to say but cannot put the words down on paper. You may get emails from professionals whose grammar and spelling are so poor you wonder how they managed to get through college.

Writing skills needed for school will be discussed in the Study Skills Unit. Below are activities you can do with your mentee to provide him opportunities to practice writing when he is with you.

Pen pals: You can help your mentee expand her knowledge of other cultures by helping her find a pen pal from another country. Teachers.net (http://teachers.net/projects/pen-pals/) is a website that posts requests from teens around the world who are looking for pen pals. Another website is My Language Exchange (http://www.mylanguageexchange.com/penpals.asp) that connects you with people from different countries who are looking for a pen pal. You can practice writing in their language, and they will practice responding in English.

Computer Skills / Word Processing: Check to see if your mentee knows basic word processing skills. If not, teach your mentee the word processing software you use. If you are not familiar with word processing software, consider taking a computer class together.

Remembrance Album: At the end of the Self-Concept and Life Success Unit, a Remembrance Album was described. Ask your mentee to write a brief paragraph describing each activity or event you recorded in the scrapbook. She could write about the location, what you did, what you saw, something funny or embarrassing that happened.

Addressing Envelopes: Students may not know how to properly address envelopes. If you need to address envelopes for a party or holiday cards, ask your mentee to help you.

Emails: Your mentee will probably have an email address. If not, look into helping him get one that is free or very low cost. During the week, you can email each other to stay in touch, confirm plans, and share how your week is going. You can email him encouraging words, funny cartoons, and items of interest to him. Email him questions that require him to reply. The point is to encourage your mentee to write.

Write for Free Stuff: One way to motivate your mentee to practice her writing skills is to write for free stuff. Caution her that she may get her name put on mailing lists and that she should not provide credit card, social security, or bank account information to anyone.

Websites for free stuff:
- Totally Free Stuff at http://www.totallyfreestuff.com/
- Free Stuff at http://www.free-stuff.com/
- Free Stuff Center at http://freestuffcenter.com/
- The Free Site at http://www.thefreesite.com/

Thank You Notes: A good habit that will earn you points in life is sending thank you notes to people who have done something special for you. A thank you is appropriate when someone gives you a gift, takes you to lunch or a movie, provides you with assistance in any form, or helps you feel better when you were sad. The note can be hand-delivered, sent by U.S. mail or email. Encourage your mentee to write thank you notes. She may need your help at first in figuring out what to write.

Planning Lists: Have your mentee write lists of food you need from the grocery store, items you have to pack for a trip, or people you want to invite to a party. If you have lots of errands to complete, ask your mentee to write them down and help you figure out a travel route to follow that will save miles and gasoline.

To Be Continued Stories: A fun activity is to write a story together. Purchase a spiral notebook. You write the first paragraph of a story or copy an opening paragraph from a book. Give the notebook to your mentee who will write the second paragraph. Keep exchanging the notebook and adding a paragraph to the story every week until you both agree that the story is complete. You can also do this by email. If you or your mentee get a hot idea for the story, don't limit yourself to one paragraph a week—just keep on writing.

UNIT THREE BIBLIOGRAPHY

Brodow, Ed. (2003). *The Forgotten Art of Listening.* http://www.hodu.com/conversation-communication.2.shtml. (accessed 6/15/05)

Burke, Ray & Herron, Ron. (1996). *Common Sense Parenting.* Boys Town, NE: Boys Town Press.

Cary, Stephen. (2000). *Working with Second Language Learners: Answers to Teachers' Top Ten Questions.* Portsmouth, New Hampshire: Heinemann.

Claire, Elizabeth. (1998). *ESL Teacher's Activities Kit.* Paramus, NJ: Prentice Hall.

Cline, Foster and Fay, Jim. (1992). *Parenting Teens With Love & Logic: Preparing Adolescents for Responsible Adulthood.* Colorado Springs, CO: Pinon Press.

Coan, Garrett. (2005). *How To Communicate Constructively.* http://www.hodu.com/constructive.shtml. (accessed 6/15/05)

Council on Interracial Books for Children. (copyright date unknown). *Guidelines for Selecting Bias-Free Textbooks and Storybooks.* New York, NY: Council on Interracial Books for Children.

Covey, Stephen R. (1989). *The Seven Habits of Highly Effective People.* New York, NY: Simon and Scheuster Publishing.

Echevarria, Jana; Vogt, Mary Ellen; Short, Deborah J. (2000). *Making Content Comprehensible for English Language Learners.* Boston, MA: Allyn and Bacon.

Echevarria, Jana and Graves, Anne. (1998). *Sheltered Content Instruction: Teaching English-Language Learners with Diverse Abilities.* Boston, MA: Allyn and Bacon.

Freeman, David E. and Yvonne S. (2001). *Between Worlds: Access to Second Language Acquisition.* Portsmouth, NH: Heinemann.

Faber, Adele and Mazlish, Elaine. (1980). *How to Talk So Kids Will Listen and Listen So Kids Will Talk.* New York, NY: Avon Books.

Ginsberg, Scott. (2005). *Why Aren't You Talking to Me?* http://www.hodu.com/not-talking.shtml. (accessed 6/15/05)

Johnston, Sue. (2005). *Yes, It's OK To Say 'No'!*
http://www.hodu.com/assertiveness-tips.shtml. (accessed 6/15/05)

Miller, Carol L. and VanDecar, Elena. (2004). *Parenting for Academic Success.* Denver, CO: Latin American Research and Service Agency.

Miller, Carol L. (1997). *Communication Skills.* Ft. Collins, CO: Jacob Center West.

Payne, Ruby K. (1998). *A Framework for Understanding Poverty.* Highlands, TX: RFT Publishing Company.

Queendom.com. (1996-2005). *Communication Skills Test—Revised.*
http://www.queendom.com/cgi-bin/tests/transfer.cgi. (accessed 6/14/05)

Seale, Doris and Slapin, Beverly. (1992). *Through Indian Eyes: The Native Experience in Books for Children.* Berkeley, Philadelphia, PA: New Society Publishers.

Sears, William and Sears, Martha. (2002). *The Successful Child: What Parents Can Do to Help Kids Turn Out Well.* Boston, MA: Little, Brown and Company.

Shapiro, Steve. (2005). "How to Listen for Success."
http://www.hodu.com/listening.shtml. (accessed 6/15/05)

Tabors, Patton O. (1997). *One Child, Two Languages: Children Learning English as a Second Language.* Baltimore, MD: Paul H. Brookes Publishing Co.

Thomson, Abrose, Angela, Chad and Greg. (1999). "A Few Simple Ideas for New Language Learners . . . And old ones needing some new life." Language Impact website. http://www.languageimpact.com/articles/gt/simple_ideas.htm. (accessed 6/22/05)

Tyler, Neal E. (1991). *Criminal Justice Academy Manual.* Pueblo, CO: Pueblo Community College.

Warfield, Anne. (2005). "Your Body Speaks Volumes, But Do You Know What It Is Saying?" http://www.dodu.com/body-language.shtml. (accessed 6/15/05)

Winless Dale, Paulette. (1998). *DID YOU SAY SOMETHING, SUSAN? How Any Woman Can Gain Confidence with Assertive Communication.* New York, NY: Carol Publishing.

UNIT FOUR: STUDY SKILLS

A.   Getting Ready to Study

      Learning Styles
      Study Skills Checklist
      Getting the Body Ready to Study
      A Good Place to Study
      Managing Study Time
      Keeping Track of Assignments
      Weekly Schedule Form

B.   Outlining / Taking Notes

      An Organized Note-taking System
      Outline Format
      Recognizing the Important Points
      Using Class Notes Effectively

C.   Reading Strategies

      The SQ3R Reading Method

D.   Writing / Editing

      Writing a Five Paragraph Essay
      Writing a Research Paper
      Editing & Proofreading
      Bibliography Resources

E.   Taking Tests

      Studying for the Test
      Test Anxiety
      Taking the Test

A. GETTING READY TO STUDY

Students need to develop good study skills in order to do well academically. Good study habits transfer and become important employability skills needed on the job.

At School	On the Job
Getting to class on time.	Getting to work on time.
Having pencil, paper, and books.	Having the tools you need.
Reading textbooks.	Reading job manuals.
Getting assignments in on time.	Meeting project deadlines.
Revising work until it's correct.	Pride in workmanship.
Time management.	Time management.
Working well in learning groups.	Good member of work team.
Organized study area.	Organized work area.

Your mentee may need your help in learning and practicing study skills that will assist him in becoming successful in life. Ask your mentee to take the *Study Skills Survey* and discuss areas he feels he needs to improve. The guidelines in this unit can be used to help him become a more skillful learner. Monitor and provide feedback and positive support as he practices these skills.

Study Skills Checklist

____ 1. I study in a place that is free from distractions and interruptions.

____ 2. Before I begin studying, I organize all the materials I need to complete my work.

____ 3. I have a system to help me keep track of my school assignments.

____ 4. I manage my time so that I can complete and turn in my assignments when they are due.

____ 5. I am able to pick out and understand the important learning points from the teacher's lecture.

____ 6. I am able to pick out and understand the important learning points from textbook assignments.

____ 7. My class and textbook notes are well organized and easy to read.

____ 8. I use my class and textbook notes to help me study for tests.

____ 9. I review my class notes regularly throughout the semester so that I do not have to cram all my studying into the evening before the test.

____ 10. I use test-taking strategies that help me do well on tests.

____ 11. I know how to access information from resources at the library.

____ 12. I know how to access information from the Internet.

____ 13. I know how to write a five-paragraph essay.

____ 14. I know how to document my sources for footnotes and bibliographies.

____ 15. I have a checklist I use to proofread my work.

____ 16. I evaluate my work to learn how to make improvements.

____ 17. I reward myself for studying hard and doing my best work.

Learning Styles

Your mentee will be a more efficient learner if she adapts her study habits to her learning style strengths. There are three basic learning styles: visual, auditory, and kinesthetic.

Auditory Learners learn information more easily when they can hear it presented; i.e., teacher lectures, audio-tapes, reading aloud, talking the topic over with others.

Visual Learners learn better when information can be read or presented in a visual format; i.e., reading books, studying pictures and graphs, reading the teacher's notes on the chalkboard, overhead screen, or in handouts.

Kinesthetic Learners learn best when they can physically manipulate something in order to learn about it; i.e., lab experiments, making models, handling actual objects instead of pictures or photos.

Ideally, teachers will use strategies that incorporate these three styles into lesson instruction so that they are teaching to the learning strengths of every student. Counsel your mentee to select classes taught by teachers whose teaching styles are a good match for her strongest learning style. Use the following suggestions to help your mentee adjust her study strategies to match her preferred learning style.

Auditory Learning Strategies

- Read your textbook aloud.
- Tape-record your notes so you can listen to them repeatedly.
- Ask the teacher if you can tape-record her lecture so you can listen to it later.
- Join a study group so you can verbally discuss the topic with others.
- Ask someone to orally quiz you on the material to be learned.

Visual Learning Strategies
- Take notes on the teacher's lecture and read them frequently.
- Take notes on the important points of textbooks you read. Read these notes often.
- Make detailed outlines for the papers you write for class.
- Draw pictures or graphs to help you visualize information.

Kinesthetic Learning Strategies
- Try to take classes that have hands-on lab components where you can actually make a project, do an experiment, or put something together while you learn.

- Put your notes on index cards so you can spread them out on the desk and manipulate them into a learning outline. Mix them up and do it again.
- Ask your teacher if you can make a display or model that demonstrates you have learned the information.
- Walk or exercise when reading or listening to your notes.

Getting the Body Ready to Study

Every person's body functions better under different conditions. Your mentee needs to figure out the physical conditions that allow him to work at his optimum. Ask him to answer these questions as they apply to him:

- Are you a morning, afternoon, or evening person? When do you have the most energy and mental alertness?
- What are your "thinking" foods? What dietary habits make you sluggish and tired? Do you eat a healthy breakfast and lunch? Or, do you skip meals and only eat "junk" food?
- Do you study with music or the TV playing? At what volume does the music and background noise become a distraction?
- Have you tried adjusting the lighting while you study? Do your eyes get tired when you read in a dark room? Does too much light create a glare that hurts your eyes?
- How many hours do you sleep each night? Do you get sleepy and tired during the day?
- How much exercise do you get each day? Do you do regular aerobic exercises to help circulate blood to your brain?

Discuss the answers to these questions with your mentee. Explain that to do his best work academically, he needs to adjust his lifestyle and environment to create the best conditions possible for studying.

A Good Place to Study

A good place to study is important to maximize the time and effort your mentee will spend on her schoolwork. Ask your mentee to evaluate the following study site descriptors to determine how she can make improvements to her study place.

- *Availability*: The site, whether it is the kitchen, bedroom, living room, or outside the home, is always available when you need to study.
- *No Distractions*: There is no loud music or TV playing, people talking or other noise that will be a distraction. People do not continually interrupt when you are studying.

- *Table/Desk Space:* There is enough surface area to spread out books, papers, and other learning materials.
- *Temperature*: The room temperature is not too hot and stuffy or too cold.
- *Lighting*: The lighting allows you to see clearly without straining or hurting your eyes.
- *Comfortable Chair*: The chair fits you well without making you too relaxed, and it provides enough comfort for long periods of studying.
- *Learning Materials:* Your study place has learning materials such as pens, paper, ruler, calculator, dictionary, and thesaurus.

If there is not an adequate place for your mentee to study in her home, help her think of alternative sites such as the library, a cyber café, the home of a friend who is a serious student, or a relative's house.

Managing Study Time

Adolescents live in the "Now" and usually do not think about or plan for the future. They will think they have plenty of time to study for next week's test or to write the term paper due next month. But there are many demands on teenagers' time. Besides school, they may be involved in extracurricular activities, have a job, or have responsibilities at home to help with chores and the care of younger siblings. Then there is social time with friends and family that needs to be squeezed into their week. Schoolwork often gets put off until the last minute, leaving little time to adequately prepare for tests and do a good job of completing class assignments. Your mentee will need your help in organizing his calendar to ensure that he schedules regular blocks of time to focus on his schoolwork.

School Year Calendar: Have your mentee write in the following dates onto a school planner or a year-at-a-glance calendar:

A. Beginning and end of the school year
B. School holidays
C. End of each grading period
D. School-wide testing days
E. Due dates for major class projects and papers
F. Final exam schedule
G. School dances and other major activities
H. Dates of important family events
I. Extracurricular activities, games, and performances

Using colored pencils that can be erased as the schedule changes is a good idea. Use different colors for school, work, family, sports, or music practices. Or try a priority system where red is used for the most important dates, green for dates of lesser importance, and blue for activities that would be nice to do but could be eliminated from the schedule in a time crunch.

Weekly Schedule: Make copies of the *Weekly Schedule* form and help your mentee make her schedule for each week. Begin by filling in the dates from the school year calendar. Then have her write in her class schedule, work hours, extracurricular activities, home chores, and eating and personal hygiene times.

Students who are overextended will often stay up late to cram in study-hours, which means they don't get enough sleep and usually results in illness, foggy thinking, and a poor attitude. These students have to prioritize their activities and make choices about what they can eliminate from their schedule. Help your mentee learn how to manage his time so that he can do his high and medium priority activities and a few on his low priority list. Point out to your mentee that school, study time, and taking care of himself physically need to be on his high priority list.

Keeping Track of Assignments

Now that your mentee has made out her weekly schedule and has set aside hours for study time, she needs to write in the specific assignments she has to complete for each class. If your mentee does not have an assignment notebook, help her develop a system for keeping track of her assignments.

After your mentee schedules time on her weekly planner to complete assignments that are due the next day or later in the week, have her write in study time to work on major projects and term papers or to review for exams that are due later in the grading period.

Keeping track of assignments may be difficult for English language learners. If your mentee is an ELL student or a person who seems to have trouble keeping assignments organized, suggest that she compare her assignment notebook with another student in her class or check with the teacher to be sure she has written down the assignments correctly.

Weekly Schedule for _____, 20___

	Sunday	Monday	Tuesday	Weds.	Thurs.	Friday	Sat.
7 am							
8 am							
9 am							
10 am							
11 am							
Noon							
1 pm							
2 pm							
3 pm							
4 pm							
5 pm							
6 pm							
7 pm							
8 pm							
9 pm							
10 pm							

B. OUTLINING / TAKING NOTES

The ability to identify and organize into outline form the important points from teacher lectures, videos, and guest speaker presentations is an important study skill. Taking good class notes will:

- Motivate you to listen more closely to what is being said.
- Help you identify the main learning points from the lecture.
- Provide you with a written record to study and help you prepare for tests.
- Record what the teacher feels is important to remember as it may be on the test.
- Provide you with information not found in the textbook.

Ask your mentee to show you her class notes. Are they sloppy and difficult to read? Are the notes well organized? Are they written in an outline format? Use the suggestions in this section to help your mentee evaluate her note taking skills.

An Organized Note Taking System

1. Use a 3-ring loose-leaf notebook with dividers to keep subjects separate.
2. Use wide-ruled 3-hole paper.
3. Write on one side of the paper only.
4. Write legibly so you and others can read your notes.
5. Keep extra paper and 1 or 2 pencils in your notebook so you are always prepared.
6. Use abbreviations that you will remember later.
7. Put teacher handouts in the notebook next to the notes for that topic.
8. Use an outline format.
9. Leave extra space so you can add information later.

Put the date, page number, and subject at the top of each page to help keep the notes organized and give you a point of reference when you need to refer back to a previous topic.

Tell your mentee to refrain from doodling on his class notes; messy notes are harder to read and will be a distraction later when he is studying his notes for the test. If there is a lull in the lecture, instead of doodling, suggest that he use this time to review and revise his notes.

Write in phrases instead of complete sentences, and use abbreviations. Information can be filled in more completely during breaks in the lecture or after class. Underline key words or highlight them with a yellow marker. Put a large asterisk (*) next to points that were emphasized by the teacher. Remember to leave empty space where you can fill in additional information at a later time.

Outline Format

Assist your mentee in organizing his notes in an outline format.

Format:
- I. Main Topic
  - A. Sub-Topic
    - I. Key Point
    - 2. Key Point
  - B. Sub-Topic
    - I. Key Point
    - 2. Key Point
    - 3. Key Point

Example:
- I. Foods of Brazil
  - A. Crops
    - I. Grains
    - 2. Fruits
    - 3. Vegetables
  - B. Animals
    - I. Cattle
    - 2. Fish
    - 3. Chickens

Recognizing the Important Points

Recognizing the main ideas in a lecture or video is key to good note taking. The following list provides guidelines to ensure that all the important learning points are recorded. Write in your notebook:

- Everything the teacher writes on the blackboard or overhead transparency.
- Anything that the teacher repeats two or more times.
- Anything the teacher says with great emphasis in his voice.
- Learning points that the teacher reviews from previous lectures.
- Information that is preceded by signal words such as:
  - "The 4 steps to . . ."
  - "The primary causes are . . ."

"An important point to remember is . . ."

- Details such as dates, names, and locations of important events.
- Equations, formulas, and graphs.
- Examples that illustrate the teacher's main points.

Remind your mentee to listen actively, be attentive, and take notes until the very end of the lecture. Suggest that she compare her notes with a student who does well on tests to see if she has missed anything important. Or, she could ask the teacher to review her notes and point out what she left out and needs to add.

Using Class Notes Effectively

Before class, complete the assigned readings and homework, review your notes from the previous class session, and be sure you have your notebook, pens, and other learning materials with you.

During class, stay focused and listen closely to what the teacher is saying. Write as quickly as you can and still be able to read your writing, using abbreviations and symbols to shorten your writing time (i.e., % for percent; # for number, & for and). Listen for the important learning points and write them into your notes. Put a question mark (?) next to those items you have questions about.

After class, as soon as possible review and revise your notes while the teacher's lecture is still fresh in your memory. Find answers to the questions you highlighted. Review your notes frequently throughout the semester.

Mentors need to check their mentee's notebook weekly to be sure he is organized and following these note-taking recommendations. You may need to help him until he becomes proficient at note-taking skills.

C. READING STRATEGIES

The ability to read and comprehend textbooks and novels increases in importance as your mentee progresses up through the middle and high school grades. Good reading skills are mandatory for academic success in college. Be sure your mentee is using the reading strategies outlined in this section. Support her in developing good reading habits by helping her apply the strategies to one or two of her reading assignments.

Before you begin, observe closely to see if your mentee has reading interference problems such as:

- English is not his first language, and his English language abilities have not developed enough for him to keep up with reading assignments.
- She has symptoms of vision problems, such as needing to hold the book close to her face when she reads, squinting or slouching, complaining of blurred vision, rereading or skipping words or sentences, or getting headaches and upset stomachs while reading.
- He has symptoms of a reading disability. He cannot seem to comprehend what he reads. A person may be able to see the words but the message is interrupted on its way to the brain, making it difficult for the person to understand what the sentence means.
- Your mentee may not have had much reading practice. Students can pass through some classes in middle and high school without ever opening their textbook. Or the student's family may not have books and other reading material in the home, because reading is not a part of the family's cultural norms.

If your mentee has any of these reading interference problems, she will need you to be patient and supportive. Work with her family, school, or local non-profit agencies to get her eyes tested for glasses or contact lenses and vision therapy. Find out what support the school provides to help her with learning disabilities. Use the techniques discussed in Unit Three: Communication Skills to help your mentee practice reading when you are together.

The SQ3R Reading Method

The SQ3R (Survey, Questions, Read, Recite, Review) reading method was developed to help students become more efficient readers and to increase their reading comprehension. Follow these directions with your mentee and help him use these strategies on his next reading assignment.

Survey

Before your mentee begins reading, have him familiarize himself with the text by looking at every page in the book. Find and read the following:

- The book and chapter titles
- Author's name and credentials. (What qualifies her to write on the subject?)
- Table of Contents
- Subheadings
- Illustrations and captions
- Graphs
- Chapter Introductions and Concluding Summaries
- End-of-chapter Questions
- Glossary
- Appendices

Question

- To provide your mentee with a reason to read and to help guide her reading, have her write down questions that she hopes the text will answer.
- Ask her to turn the title, headings and subheadings into 'who, what, where, why, when and how' questions. For example, if the heading was *Getting Ready To Study*, she would ask herself, "What do I have to do to get ready to study?"
- Most texts have study questions for each chapter. Have your mentee go over these questions before she begins reading.

Read

- Have your mentee read each section of the chapter to find answers to the questions he developed and the study questions located at the beginning or end of the chapter.
- Have him write the questions and answers in his text notes.
- He needs to read the captions under the illustrations; study the graphs and charts; and pay close attention to italicized and bolded words and phrases.
- If the section is difficult to understand, have him reduce his speed and reread the information.
- Ask him to write down words he does not understand. Have a dictionary close by so he can look up the words and add them to his vocabulary-building list.

Recite

- Read the text questions aloud and orally answer these questions. Your mentee can do this by herself, with a study partner, or with you.
- She will be able to retain the information better when she *reads, says, hears, and writes the answers.*

Review

- Your mentee needs to combine his text notes with his class lecture notes by subject heading so that he can review them together.
- He can use the learning style strategies described earlier in this unit to study his notes.
- He will retain the information better if he reviews his text and class notes during several short 15-minute periods rather than one long 2-hour study session.
- He can review his notes while standing in lines, waiting for classes to start, or riding to school.
- Your mentee needs to schedule review sessions into his weekly planner.

D. WRITING AND EDITING

In 2004, the National Commission on Writing surveyed major American corporations to determine the importance of writing skills for employment. The Commission found that people who cannot write and communicate clearly will not be hired and are unlikely to last long enough to be considered for promotion. One survey respondent said, "In most cases, writing ability could be your ticket in . . . or it could be your ticket out." College instructors are appalled at the poor writing skills of incoming freshmen students. Expressing yourself through good writing skills is important for success in school and at work.

Writing for School and on the Job
- Applications for jobs, colleges, and scholarships may be discounted or ignored if the writing is messy and illegible.
- Many college and scholarship applications require a written essay to be mailed with the application form.
- Statewide high stakes achievement tests frequently include a writing section.
- Secondary and post-secondary classes give essay question tests.
- Secondary and post-secondary classes require students to write reports, essays, and research papers.
- Employees must write accurate and clearly understood reports.
- Employees need to write good business letters.

Discuss the importance of good writing skills with your mentee. Explain how you use these skills at your job. Students will be more motivated to learn and practice writing skills if they understand how the skills will benefit them later.

Writing a Five-Paragraph Essay

Your mentee may ask you to help her write or proofread her essay for English class. Ask your mentee to let you read the essay format instructions her teacher is requiring her to follow. If your mentee does not have written instructions from her teacher, use the following standard essay format.

Paragraph 1: Introduce the essay subject with a general topic sentence. Provide a brief summary of the supporting subtopics to be covered in paragraphs 2, 3, and 4.

Paragraph 2: Restate subtopic #1 and provide supporting details or examples.

Paragraph 3: Restate subtopic #2 and provide supporting details or examples.

Paragraph 4: Restate subtopic #3 and provide supporting details or examples.

Paragraph 5: Close with a paragraph that rephrases the main topic and subtopics as a summary or conclusion.

Read and discuss the five-paragraph essay, "Save Time By Getting Ready to Study," with your mentee. Identify the main topic, subtopics, and supporting details.

Sample 5-paragraph Essay

Save Time By Getting Ready to Study

1. "The test is on Friday, and I need to study—but I don't have time!" When time is limited because of obligations such as a part-time job and soccer practice everyday after school, making the best use of study time is important. Organizing your work area, having materials readily available, and being mentally alert ensures that time set aside for studying is used effectively. Getting ready to study actually saves time.

2. The first step in getting ready to study is to organize the work area. A good place to study is free of distractions and interruptions. The television is turned off; music is played at a volume that does not interfere; and telephone calls are answered by voice mail and returned later. There is a flat, clean surface such as a desk or table where learning materials can be spread out for easy access. There is good lighting, and the room temperature is adjusted for maximum comfort without making you sleepy.

3. The next step is to collect everything that will be needed for studying. The basics include paper, pens, pencils, calculator, and a dictionary. And, of course, textbooks, class notes, and any other resources needed to complete the assignments must be available at your fingertips. A lot of time is wasted when you have to interrupt your studying to look for these materials.

4. The study place is ready, and all the materials are collected. The final step is getting you ready. Time spent studying is more effective when you are in your best physical condition. Getting adequate rest, eating a nutritious diet, and exercising to circulate the blood to your brain are important for mental alertness. It's also important to avoid using drugs and alcohol that will dull your thinking. A person is able to think more clearly and for longer periods of time when they are in good physical shape.

5. When time for homework and preparing for the test is limited, save time by getting ready to study. Before you start your study session, arrange the study area for optimal conditions and few interruptions; gather all the materials needed; and get in good physical shape so you'll be mentally alert. Following these study tips will ensure that the time you have set aside for studying is used wisely.

Writing a Research Paper

Writing a research paper cannot be put off until the night before it is due. Be sure your mentee has scheduled time in his monthly and weekly planners to accomplish the following steps for writing a research paper.

1. *Select a Topic.* If the teacher has not assigned a topic for the paper, help your mentee select a topic that will be of interest to her and one that is not too broad. For example, "Mexico" as a topic is too broad. The topic needs to be narrowed down to a subject that can be researched and written about in a space the length of her term paper; i.e., "Museums of Mexico City" or "Hurricanes on the Mexican Pacific Coast."

2. *Locate Information Resources.* Find information about the topic in library resources such as books on the subject, encyclopedias, atlases, magazines, and videos. Conduct an Internet search.

3. *Prepare Bibliography Cards.* For every resource used, write the source's bibliographic information on a separate note card. Use the teacher's required bibliography format.

4. *Make Note Cards.* Write down information about the subject on note cards that can be arranged later into an outline for the paper.

5. *Develop An Outline.* Arrange your information note cards into an outline by subtopics. "Hurricanes on the Mexican Pacific Coast" could be arranged chronologically or by the intensity of the storms. "Museums of Mexico City" could be arranged by size, subject, or geographic location.

6. *Write a Rough Draft.* Using your outline and note cards, write the first draft of the paper.

7. *Proofread and Revise the Rough Draft.* Using the proofreading tips on the following page, check your work and make the necessary revisions.

8. *Prepare Bibliography.* Using the bibliography note cards, type a bibliography in the format provided by the teacher.

9. *Title Page and Table of Contents.* The title page is the first page and includes the title of the paper, the class, teacher's name, date the paper is due, and your mentee's name as the author. The Table of Contents is the second page and provides a list

of main topics, subtopics, any graphs or tables, and the bibliography along with the corresponding page numbers.

10. *Make a Copy of Your Paper*: Have your mentee make a zerox copy of his paper before he turns it into the teacher. Lost papers are hard to re-create from memory.

Editing and Proofreading

After completing the written assignment, help your mentee proofread, edit, and revise the paper until she feels the essay or research paper represents her best effort. Use the following proofreading list to help her check her work.

Proofreading Checklist
- Used the teacher-required format.
- Wrote the required number of pages.
- Used double-spaced lines.
- Used one inch margins.
- Wrote on one side of paper only.
- Wrote in pen or typed.
- Page numbers in correct place on page.
- Placed in folder or stabled in top left hand corner.
- Placed a title at top of first page.
- Included a table of contents.
- Checked for spelling errors.
- Checked for correct grammar and punctuation.
- Eliminated run-on or incomplete sentences.
- Words are capitalized as needed.
- An outside person has proofread the paper.

Bibliography

If the teacher does not provide a format for writing bibliographic references, the info. please website provides guidelines and examples to follow. The website address is: http://www.infoplease.com/homework/t8biblio.html.

Jo Ann Klassen, Media Specialist at Cedaroak Park Elementary School in West Linn, Oregon has developed an excellent bibliography citation work-sheet available at http://www.oslis.k12.or.us/elementary/howto/cited/ on the Internet.

E. TAKING TESTS

Testing is a strong part of 21st century culture. We take entrance exams to get into college; placement tests are administered for employment; tests must be passed to be licensed to drive or to practice certain professions. To graduate from high school, your mentee will have to demonstrate his knowledge by passing many tests during his middle and high school years. Test taking is a skill that must be learned and practiced. You can help your mentee become proficient at taking tests by sharing the suggestions provided in this section.

Studying for the Test

Unless your mentee has a photographic memory, he will need to study to do well on tests. The following strategies may help:

1. Get your mind focused. Be alert. Avoid distractions.
2. Use positive self-talk to remind you of the importance of studying so you can pass the test.
3. Create your own incentive or reward for sticking with your studies. Knowing you will allow yourself a special treat helps keep you going.
4. Gather all your materials before you begin: old quizzes and tests, class notes, text notes, and teacher handouts.
5. Vary your study strategies. Use the auditory, visual, and kinesthetic strategies described previously.
6. Study the subjects that are more difficult for you when you have the most energy.
7. Schedule frequent short review sessions the week before the test.
8. Consider studying with a friend or friends who are serious students.
9. Take regular study breaks.
10. Stay in good physical shape so you are functioning at your best. Get adequate sleep; eat healthy foods; and exercise to get your blood circulating.

Text Anxiety

Most everyone gets nervous or hyped when they have to take a test. If your mentee's test anxiety is too high, her test performance may be negatively affected. To help her reduce test anxiety, suggest the following:

1. Know the learning material well. Study and frequently review your class notes,

text notes, quizzes, tests, and teacher handouts. Being prepared boosts your self-confidence.

2. Get a good night's sleep the day before the test. Eat a nutritious breakfast and lunch.
3. Get to class early so you don't feel rushed and flustered.
4. Take a watch or sit where you can see a wall clock so your can keep track of the time.
5. Take extra pens and pencils and any other equipment you are allowed to use.
6. Use positive self-talk. Give yourself "I can do this" messages.
7. Take a few deep, relaxing breaths. Focus your attention on the task at hand.

Taking the Test

I. Be sure your name is on the test.
2. Read the directions carefully. Ask the teacher if you don't understand the directions.
3. Review the entire test first. Decide how much time you can spend on each section of the test. Keep track of the time to be sure you can finish answering all the questions.
4. Read each question carefully.
5. Answer the easy questions that you know first and then work on the harder questions.
6. When you are finished, review the questions and answers for accuracy and completeness.
7. Keep your eyes on your own work so the teacher will not suspect you of cheating.

There are several websites listed in the bibliography that will provide your mentee with additional tips for taking objective and essay tests. Suggest that she look them up on the Internet. Use these search words: test-taking strategies.

UNIT FOUR: BIBLIOGRAPHY

Canter, Lee and Housner, Lee. (1987). *Homework Without Tears.* New York, NY: Harper & Row.

College Tutorials: Writing and Editing Your Term Papers and Essays. http://college-tutorials.hodu.com/termpapers-outline.shtml (accessed on 6/15/05)

"Cook Counseling Center Study Skills Inventory." (2000). Blacksburg, VA: Virginia Tech Division of Student Affairs. http://www.ucc.vt.edu/studyskills/aassaform.htm. (accessed on 5/10/05)

Ellis, David B. (1981). *Survival Tools for College.* Rapid City, SD: College Survival, Inc.

Hansen, Randall and Katharine, "The Importance of Good Writing Skills." Indispensable Writing Resources. http://www.quintcareers.com/writing/skills.html. (accessed on 7/1/05)

Heacox, Diane. (1991). *Up From Underachievement.* Minneapolis, MN: Free Spirit Publishing Inc.

How-To-Study.Com: A Study Skills Resource Site. http://www.how-to-study.com/. (accessed on 6/27/05)

Infoplease: All the Knowledge You Need. "How to Write a Five Paragraph Essay." http://www.infoplease.com/homework/wsfivepara.html. (accessed on 7/1/05)

Infoplease: All the Knowledge You Need. "How to Write a Research Paper." http://www.infoplease.com/homework/t8biblio.thml. (accessed on 7/1/05)

Landsberger, Joe. (1996). "Study Guides & Strategies." St. Paul, Minnesota. http://www.studygs.net.htm. (accessed on 5/19/05)

"Lecture Note Taking." St. Joseph's, MN: College of Saint Benedict / Saint John's University. http://www.csbsju.edu/academicadvising/help/lec-note.htm. (accessed on 5/10/05)

Miller, Carol and VanDecar, Elena. (2004). *Parenting for Academic Success.* Denver, CO: Latin American Research and Service Agency.

National Commission on Writing: "Writing: A Ticket to Work... Or a Ticket Out. A Survey of Business Leaders." (2004). http://www.writingcommission.org/prod_downloads/writingcom/writing-ticket-to-work.pdf (accessed on 7/1/05)

Oregon School Library Information System: How to Cite Sources. http://www.oslis.k12.or.us/elementary/howto/cited/. (accessed on 7/01/05)

Robinson, Francis Pleasant. (1961, 1970). *Effective Study* (4th ed.), New York, NY: Harper & Row.

The Study Center: Academic Support Services for Students. Baltimore, MA: Loyola College. (accessed on 5/10/05)

Teaching Today, (2000-2005). "Writing Skills." New York, NY: Glencoe/McGraw-Hill. http://www.glencoe.com/sec/teachingtoday/tiparchive.phtml/9 (accessed on 7/1/05)

UNIT FIVE: LIFE SKILLS

A. Physical Health
    Physical Activity
    Nutrition
    Hygiene
    Smoking
    Alcohol and Drug Abuse
    Sexually Transmitted Diseases & AIDS/HIV

B. Mental Health
    Stress Management
    Anger Management
    Eating Disorders
    Depression
    Suicide

C. Safety
    Safety at Home
    Safety on the Street
    Safety in the Car
    Safety Riding Your Bicycle
    Safety Using the Internet
    Safety on Dates
    Calling 911
    Teens and Safety Websites

D. Relationships
    Healthy vs. Unhealthy Relationships
    Establishing Healthy Boundaries
    Sexual Harassment
    Conflict Resolution
    Prejudice and Discrimination

E. Decision Making
G. Civic Responsibility
H. Goal Setting

A. PHYSICAL HEALTH

Many teens today have developed poor lifestyle habits that negatively affect their health. They don't eat a nutritious, balanced diet; they spend too little time on physical activities, opting instead for sitting in front of the television or computer for hours at a time; and some youth smoke, drink, or use illegal drugs. As a mentor, you can encourage your mentee to develop and practice habits that promote good physical health. Remind them that being in excellent physical condition helps them to look and feel their best and promotes mental alertness needed to do well in school and on the job.

Physical Activity

The U.S. Department of Health and Human Services recommends that children and teens get 60 minutes of physical activity every day of the week to promote cardio-respiratory function, blood pressure control, weight management, and cognitive and emotional well-being. The Department states that, "childhood and adolescence are pivotal times for preventing sedentary behavior among adults by maintaining the habit of physical activity throughout the school years." Encourage your mentee to get involved in physical activities by joining her in an aerobics class, hiking, skating, swimming, dancing, and so forth. You can have fun together while you exercise.

Nutrition

The U.S. Department of Agriculture's *Dietary Guidelines for Americans, 2005* states that healthy eating includes making smart choices from every food group, finding a balance between food intake and physical activity, and getting the most nutrition out of your calories. The Guidelines describe a healthy diet as one that:

- Emphasizes fruits, vegetables, whole grains, and fat-free or low-fat milk and milk products;
- Includes lean meats, poultry, fish, beans, eggs, and nuts; and
- Is low in saturated fats, trans fats, cholesterol, salt (sodium) and added sugars.

One way to determine if you are making healthy food choices is to check the Nutrition Facts label on packaged foods.

Understanding Nutrition Facts Labels

The federal government requires that most packaged foods list Nutrition Facts on the label of the container. All labels must provide the same information and conform to the same format. The chart below lists the Nutrition Facts of two different snack products.

Nutrition Facts

1 oz. Serving	Label A	Label B
Serving Size	1 package-1 oz.	1 oz.—28 g—¼ cup
Servings per container	1	10
Calories per serving	120	170
Calories from fat	15	140
Total fat	2 grams—3%	16 grams—25%
Saturated fat	0 grams—0%	2 grams—10%
Cholesterol	0 grams—0%	0 grams—0%
Sodium	70 grams—3%	140 grams—6%
Total Carbohydrates	23 grams—8%	6 grams—2%
Dietary Fiber	1 gram—6%	3 grams—12%
Sugars	15 grams	1 gram
Protein	2 grams	6 grams
Vitamin A	0%	0%
Vitamin C	0%	0%
Calcium	0%	6%
Iron	0%	6%

1. *Serving Size and Servings Per Container*: Label A has one serving per container and the serving size is one ounce. Label B has ten servings per container and a serving size is 1 ounce or about 1/4 cup. If you eat the entire container of the Label B food, you must multiply the grams and percentage amounts given for each nutrient by ten. For example, Label B sodium content for one serving is 140 milligrams. If you eat the entire container, you must multiply 140 mg by 10, which means you have eaten 1400 milligrams of sodium—more than half the daily recommended amount of sodium intake.

2. *Nutritional Content:* The Food and Drug Administration has established the following criteria for determining "healthy" food:

    • Must be low in fat and saturated fat.
    • Contain limited amounts of cholesterol and sodium.
    • Provide at least 10% of one or more of vitamins A or C, iron, calcium, protein or fiber.
    • Sodium content cannot exceed 360 mg per individual serving.

Next to the fat, cholesterol, sodium, carbohydrates, dietary fiber, sugar and protein items are the gram amounts contained in a single serving and the percentage of USDA recommended daily intake for each of these items. Study Labels A and B with your mentee and decide which is the healthier food item.

If you are on a low carb, high fiber diet, Label B is the choice for you even though the fat content is high. If you are on a low fat or low sodium diet, eat Label A, noting that this food serving contains 15 grams of sugar.

3.   *Vitamins and Minerals*: The label must list the percentages of Vitamins A and C, iron and calcium contained in one serving. Notice that the percentages for Label A are all zero, meaning that this food does not meet the healthy foods criteria. Two servings of Label B would provide the 10% amounts of vitamins and minerals required by the FDA guidelines; however, two servings will bring the fat content up to 50%.

Study the Nutrition Facts labels with your mentee when you grocery shop or decide what you want to eat for snacks. If you go online, most fast food restaurants will provide this information for their menu items.

Healthy Eating Reminders
- Try to eat three balanced meals plus two nutritious snacks each day. If you are not going to be home, take a healthy snack to eat while you're out.
- Limit the amount of fast food and high sugar content foods you eat.
- Eat when you are hungry; stop eating when you feel full.
- Instead of deep-frying food (like fast food places do), prepare your food by baking, broiling, grilling, or microwaving.
- Limit toppings like butter, margarine, or gravy. Try using fat-free seasonings like herbs, garlic, chili powder, and pepper to add taste to your food.
- Do not drink more than one can of sugar pop or juice a day. These drinks are high in calories and low or empty in nutritional value.
- Eat slowly and chew your food well.
- If you eat when you are stressed-out, try other relaxation techniques instead.

When you and your mentee are eating out, preparing meals, or planning snacks, use the eating guidelines in this section to help you choose healthy foods. When you are on field trips together or during study sessions, instead of buying snacks at a fast food place or convenience store, take healthy snacks with you like fresh or dried fruit, cut-up fresh vegetables, string cheese, unsalted nuts, yogurt, 100% juice boxes or bottles, herbal tea, or whole-wheat pretzels.

Hygiene

A young person's body undergoes many physical changes during adolescents. Changes in hormones and an increase in body size require your mentee to practice different hygiene routines. If your mentee's appearance is unkempt or her body odor is unpleasant, advise her that as she transitions into adulthood, she needs to make changes in her hygiene habits. You can suggest that she refer to the following list to remind her of daily hygiene practices to use.

1. Shampoo your hair daily or every other day. Use a conditioner if desired. Use "greaseless" or "oil free" styling gels.
2. Bathe or shower everyday using a mild soap. In hot, sticky weather or after a hard day of physical labor, you may need to shower more often to stay fresh.
3. Wear clean clothes, socks, and underwear every day.
4. Consider using an underarm deodorant with an antiperspirant that helps keep you from perspiring.
5. Brush your teeth at least twice a day. Floss your teeth daily to remove plaque from between your teeth.
6. If possible, get your teeth cleaned and checked by a dentist twice a year.
7. Use mouth guards to protect your teeth when playing sports.
8. Don't smoke. Smoking stains your teeth, gives you bad breath, and leads to oral cancer and gum disease.
9. Reconsider if you decide to have your tongue pierced. Oral piercing can cause infections, bleeding, and nerve damage. You can choke on studs and barbells that come loose, and metal jewelry can chip or crack your teeth and damage your gums.
10. Promote a good complexion, shiny hair, and a radiant smile by eating a healthy, nutritious diet.

Smoking

The American Lung Association reports that 1/3 of all smokers had their first cigarette by the age of 14. Ninety percent of all smokers began before the age of 21. If your mentee smokes or tells you he is being pressured to smoke by his friends, share with him the following negative effects of smoking.

Harmful to Your Body

A. Can cause cancer of the lungs, mouth, throat, bladder, pancreas, and kidneys.
B. Causes gum disease.
C. Increases your heart rate and blood pressure.
D. Can lead to heart disease and strokes.
E. Makes breathing more difficult.
F. Lessens the blood and oxygen flow to your muscles.
G. Increases the number of colds you get each year.
H. Makes you cough and wheeze.
I. Weakens your bones.

Detracts from Your Physical Appearance

- Dries out your skin and causes wrinkles.
- Yellows your teeth and stains your lips.
- Gives you bad breath.
- Can lead to premature gray hair and hair loss.
- Makes your skin, hair, and clothes smell badly.

Smoking Is Addictive

As the nicotine in tobacco goes through your bloodstream and to your brain, you initially feel good. However, in less than an hour these good feelings go away and you start to feel nervous or moody and your brain begins to crave more nicotine. The younger you are when you start smoking, the more likely you are to become strongly addicted.

Smoking Is Expensive

The price of cigarettes has increased significantly over the past decade. Smoking is an expensive habit to maintain. There are better and healthier ways for teens to spend their money.

Your second-hand smoke is dangerous for your friends and family to breathe.

SMOKING CAN KILL YOU!!!

If your mentee smokes and is ready to quit, there are resources available to help her.

- Call the local chapter of the American Lung Association, the local hospital, or health department and ask about programs to help teens quit smoking.
- Have your mentee check with the school counselor or nurse for referrals to programs to help him quit.
- Look up the following excellent websites for information and assistance:

Not-On-Tobacco (N-O-T), American Lung Association Program. www.lungusa.org
I QUIT! National Center for Chronic Disease Prevention and Health Promotion. http://www.cdc.gov/tobacco/quit.htm
A Breath of Fresh Air! Independence From Smoking—for Teens, National Women's Health Information Center. www.4woman.gov/QuitSmoking/index.cfm
Online Guide to Quitting. www.Smokefree.gov
How Can I Quit Smoking? www.kidshealth.org/teen/drug_alcohol/tobacco/quit_smoking.html
Campaign for Tobacco-Free Kids. www.tobaccofreekids.org

KEEPKIDSFROMSMOKING.com

Tobacco Information and Prevention Source (TIPS) Center for Disease Control. www.cdc.gov

National Center for Tobacco Free Kids, American Heart Association http://www.amhrt.org

Sport Initiatives—Tobacco Free Sports. www.cdc.gov/tobacco/sports_initiatives_splash.htm

National Cancer Institute Hotline to talk to a counselor at 877-448-7848.

Alcohol and Drug Abuse

Teenagers in every community can easily access alcohol and illegal drugs. Beer, wine, liquor, marijuana, and other drugs are available at their schools and jobs, parties they attend, and the alleys and parks where they hang out. The American Academy of Child and Adolescent Psychiatry developed a list of warning signs that indicate a teenager may be abusing drugs and alcohol. If your mentee is exhibiting some of these symptoms, you need to take action to ensure that he gets the help he needs.

Warning Signs of Teenage Alcohol and Drug Abuse

Physical:	Fatigue, sleep problems, repeated health complaints, red and glazed eyes, and a lasting cough.
Emotional:	Personality change, sudden mood changes, irritability, irresponsible behavior, low self-esteem, poor judgment, depression, withdrawal, and a general lack of interest.
Family:	Starting arguments, breaking rules, or withdrawing from family.
School:	Decreased interest in school, negative attitude, drop in grades, many absences, truancy, and discipline problems.
Social:	Peer group involved with drugs and alcohol, problems with the law, dramatic changes in dress and appearance.

Get the Facts

If you believe your mentee has a drug or alcohol problem or if she comes to you asking for help for herself or a friend, the first step is to get accurate information. The following websites have been developed by experts in the field of drug and alcohol addiction and education. These organizations provide information on medical research, statistical data, descriptions of the effects of alcohol, legal and illegal drug abuse, prevention strategies, and intervention techniques designed especially for teens. Spend time with your mentee browsing these websites. Discuss what you learn. Your mentee needs accurate information to help her make good life decisions.

Drug and Alcohol Information Websites

- 4 Girls Health. http://www.4girls.gov/substance/alcohol.htm
- Al-Anon/Alateen. http://www.al-anon.alateen.org/
- American Academy of Child & Adolescent Psychiatry, Teens: Alcohol and other Drugs. http://www.aacap.org/publications/factsfam/teendrug.htm
- American Council for Drug Education. http:www.acde.org
- BAM! Body and Mind, Center for Disease Control website for teens. http://www.bam.gov/flash_elli.html
- Drug and Alcohol Treatment and Prevention Global Network http://www.drug-net.net
- NIDA for Teens, National Institute on Drug Abuse. http://teens.drugabuse.gov/
- Partnership for a Drug-Free America. http://www.drugfree.org
- PREVLINE: Prevention Online. http://www.health.org/
- Substance Abuse & Mental Health Services Administration (SAMHSA). United States Department of Health and Human Services. http://www.samhsa.gov
- TeensHealth, KidsHealth Website. http://www.kidshealth.org/teen/drug_alcohol

Drug / Alcohol Abuse Intervention Strategies

If you feel your mentee is abusing alcohol or drugs, implement some of the following strategies when you are together. Consider discussing your concerns with your mentee's family or school counselor. If possible, form a team approach to intervention.

1. *Early and Continuing Education.* Use the websites listed above or look for community resources to help provide you and your mentee with current and accurate information regarding alcohol and drug abuse. Drug and alcohol education needs to be an ongoing process.

2. *Open Communication*: Keep the lines of communication open; look for verbal and non-verbal communication cues; listen well to what your mentee is telling you. Look for opportunities to discuss your concerns with him.

3. *Positive Role Modeling*: Do not use illegal drugs. If you drink, do so in moderation and responsibly but never drink alcoholic beverages when your mentee is with you.

4. *Refusal Techniques*: Model for and discuss refusal techniques—words to use when you want to say "no" to offers of drugs or alcohol.

5. *Safety Rules*: Talk with your mentee's family about establishing safety rules when going out with friends.
   - Don't drive when you have been drinking or ride with someone who has been drinking.
   - Have a cell phone or money to pay for a call when you need to come home or leave a situation.
   - Keep your drink in your hand to be sure no one puts alcohol or drugs in it. If you put your drink down without watching it, throw it out and get a new drink.
   - Let your family know where you'll be, give them a contact number, and call them if your plans change.
   - Let teens know you expect them to leave when the situation gets dangerous.

6. *Self-Esteem Building*: Teens who abuse alcohol and drugs tend to have low self-esteem. Use the strategies and activities outlined in Unit Two: Self-Concept and Life Success to help improve your mentee's self-esteem.

7. *Decision-Making Skills*: Use the decision-making model discussed later in this unit to help your mentee learn and practice how to make good decisions.

8. *Goal Setting*: Encourage your mentee to make both short- and long-term goals for himself. Discuss how drug and alcohol abuse are barriers that will prevent him from attaining his goals.

9. *Drug/Alcohol Free Activities:* Help your mentee plan activities with her friends that will be drug and alcohol-free. If her friends are not interested in joining her, suggest that she find new friends who are committed to a drug/alcohol-free lifestyle.

10. *Negative Effects*: Use news items on television or in the newspaper or the irresponsible behavior of friends and acquaintances to discuss the negative impact of drug and alcohol abuse on themselves and others.

11. *Community Resources*: If your mentee or his family decides that he needs intervention and treatment, help them find resources in the community such as Alateen and AA meetings and treatment programs.

Sexually Transmitted Diseases and AIDS/HIV

The Center for Disease Control reports that of the 19 million sexually transmitted disease (STDs) infections that occur annually in the United States, almost half of these are among youth ages 15 to 24. The Kaiser Family Foundation's *2000 National Survey of Teens on HIV/AIDS* reported that:

- People under the age of 25 make up half of all new HIV infections occurring in the U.S.
- Teen girls account for 58% of new AIDS cases reported among young people ages 13-19.
- African American teens represent 60% of new AIDS cases reported among those ages 13-19.
- Latino teens represent 24% of new cases for this age group.

The seriousness of this reality means that education about and treatment for STDs and HIV/AIDS cannot be ignored or minimized. Your role as a mentor is to ensure that your mentee has accurate information regarding STDs and HIV/AIDS, to answer his questions when they arise, and to help him find health resources in his community for testing and treatment, if needed.

The American Academy of Family Physicians in their website article, "Talking to Your Child About STDs," recommends:

- Begin discussions regarding STDs during the child's preteen and middle school years.
- When your child asks questions about STDs and HIV/AIDS, use this opportunity to discuss and find out what she needs to know to help keep her safe and free from disease.
- Use media cues, like a TV program or a newspaper article, to lead into a discussion about STDs.
- Ask her what she already knows about STDs and HIV/AIDS. What else does she want to know? What questions does she have? Answer her questions honestly.
- Discuss sexual scenes in movies and on TV. Use these stories to lead into a conversation about safe sex and risky behavior.
- Obtain literature to inform yourself and your mentee on STDs and HIV/AIDS from your doctor, health department, or local Planned Parenthood office.
- Read the following websites with your mentee:

  - www.riskystuff.com
  - Teens Health at http://kidshealth.org
  - Free Teens at http://www.freeteens.org/
  - CDC STD Prevention at http://www.cdc.gov/nchstp
  - www.iwannaknow.org
  - teenwire.com
  - Health Pages at http://www.thehealthpages.com
  - National STD Hotline at 1-800-227-8922

B. MENTAL HEALTH

Stress Management

Stress is the body's natural reaction to tension, pressure, and change. Teenagers experience stress from many sources:

- Demands of school and jobs
- Changes in their bodies
- Problems with family and friends
- Separation or divorce of parents
- Death of a loved one
- Living in an unsafe environment
- Chronic illness in the family
- Moving or changing schools
- Too many demands on their time
- Family financial problems
- Peer pressure
- Feeling lonely and left out

Not all stress is bad. Nervous tension before a sports competition, final exam, speech, or musical recital may give you an extra adrenalin boost to help you perform better. However, stress overload can result in negative physical and mental effects, and prolonged stress can lead to serious health problems.

Symptoms of Stress

Physical: Headaches, nervousness, rashes, stomachaches, rapid heartbeat, perspiration, lack of energy

Mental: Lack of concentration, forgetfulness, a drop in school performance, unable to study, carelessness

Emotional: Bored, irritable, nightmares, sad/depressed, scared, withdrawn, trouble sleeping, laughing or crying for no reason, anxious

If your mentee has symptoms of being on stress overload, encourage her to try some of the following stress management strategies.

Stress Management Strategies

- Exercise and eat regularly.
- Avoid excess caffeine, illegal drugs, alcohol, and tobacco.
- Learn and use relaxation exercises such as deep breathing and muscle relaxing techniques.
- Decrease negative self-talk and replace your deflating messages with encouraging, self-affirming words.
- Take breaks from stressful situations and do activities that you enjoy.
- Build a network of friends, both peers and adults, who will listen and help you cope in positive ways.
- Learn practical coping skills; i.e., time management, organizational skills, breaking large tasks into smaller, easier ones.
- Stop worrying about things that may never happen. Focus on what you need to get done today, in this hour.
- Ask for help when you get too overwhelmed, or decide what you can cross off your to-do list until you have more time.
- Say "no" to others' requests that will add to your stress level.
- Laugh or cry. Both reactions alleviate stress.
- Reward yourself for your hard work and efforts. Even if you don't hear the words from anyone else, you can tell yourself, "Well done! You're doing a good job!"

Anger Management

Teenagers get angry; it is a normal emotion. They get stressed out, have mood swings caused by hormone changes, feel a lack of control over their lives, and alternate between acting like a child and a more mature young adult. If your mentee gets angry frequently or you think he will benefit from some anger management instruction, use the information in this section to jump-start your conversations with him regarding his anger problems.

In their book, *Letting Go of Anger*, Ron and Pat Potter-Efron describe seven characteristics of healthy anger management.

1. Anger is treated as a normal part of life.
2. Anger is used as a signal that the person has problems that need to be addressed.
3. Anger is acted upon only after a person has carefully thought through the situation.
4. Anger is expressed in moderation, without the person losing control.
5. The goal of anger management is to solve problems, not just to vent emotions.
6. The person uses "I" messages to state clearly why they are angry. They communicate in a manner that will help others understand and respond to their concerns appropriately.

7. The person releases their anger and moves on once the problem has been resolved.

When your mentee gets angry, encourage her to calm down and take time to think before she does or says anything. Ask her to identify the problem and determine specifically what it is that has made her angry. The next step is to think of solutions to the problem and what the consequences of each potential solution might be. Then select a solution and put it into action.

Healthy Outlets for Anger
- Listen to music (with your headphones on) and dance with anger-inspired energy.
- Write out your angry feelings in your journal.
- Draw out your anger by scribbling, doodling, and sketching.
- Work out your anger by playing a sport or running.
- Talk about your feelings with someone you trust.
- Distract yourself to get your mind off the situation by watching TV, reading, playing video games, etc.
- Go somewhere by yourself and scream out your anger.
- Pound your pillow or throw rocks into a lake.

Remind your mentee that healthy expressions of anger mean that no one gets hurt physically or emotionally. Also remind him that expressing his anger and calming down is only the first step in resolving the situation that created his anger. He will still need to work on solutions. Decision-making and problem-solving skills are discussed later in this unit.

Eating Disorders

Eating disorders are defined by the National Institute of Mental Health as "any serious disturbance in eating behavior such as extreme and unhealthy reduction of food intake or severe overeating, as well as feelings of distress or extreme concern about body shape or weight." Eating disorders are treatable medical illnesses and need to be taken seriously as they can be life threatening.

Possible Causes of Eating Disorders

Scientific research is ongoing to determine the causal factors of eating disorders. Any one or a combination of the following conditions may contribute to the development of an eating disorder.

- Living in a culture that promotes an unrealistic body shape. Media advertisements, magazines, the food industry, and peers put pressure on teens to be unnaturally thin.

- Participating in a sport such as gymnastics, dance, ballet, or skating that emphasizes thinness.
- Suffering from a psychological or mood disorder such as depression or obsessive/compulsive disorder.
- Desiring to exercise rigid control over one's life to compensate for feelings of sadness and anxiety.
- Having a strong need to be and look "perfect."
- Living in a stressful family situation.
- Dealing with a difficult transition or loss.

If your mentee has an obsession with weight and food, needs to exercise all the time even when she's exhausted, wears only baggy clothes, takes diet pills or laxatives, or avoids eating when she is with you, she may have an eating disorder that requires treatment.

There are three main eating disorders: anorexia nervosa, bulimia nervosa, and binge-eating disorder. Become familiar with the symptoms of these disorders to help determine if your mentee suffers from any of them and may need your help.

Anorexia Nervosa
- Resistance to maintaining body weight at or above a normal weight for age and height. Person will compulsively exercise or purge by vomiting or abusing laxatives, enemas, and diuretics in order to rid her body of calorie intake.
- Intense fear of gaining weight or becoming fat.
- Inaccurate perception of their body shape. People see themselves as "fat" even though they are actually dangerously thin.
- Infrequent or absent menstrual periods.

A person with anorexia may have dizziness, heart problems, low blood pressure, low body temperature, and fainting spells. Other symptoms include dry skin, dehydration, constipation, and depression. People can die from complications of anorexia that result in cardiac arrest, electrolyte imbalance, or suicide.

Bulimia Nervosa
- Recurrent episodes of binge-eating where people eat an excessive amount of food within a limited period of time and feel a lack of control over their eating.
- Prevents weight gain by self-induced vomiting, misuse of laxatives, diuretics, and enemas, fasting or excessive exercise.
- Binge eating episodes and purging behaviors occur at least twice a week over a three-month period.

A person with bulimia may have a normal weight and will often binge-eat and purge in secret, so it may be difficult to know if they are bulimic. They may suffer from serious electrolyte problems, irregular menstrual periods, dehydration, swollen face, sore throat, tooth decay, dry, flaky skin, constant upset stomach, heartburn, constipation, depression, and low potassium levels from vomiting. Bulimia can cause permanent damage to teeth, bowels, stomach, heart, nerves, and metabolism.

Binge-Eating Disorder
- Eating more rapidly than normal.
- Eating until feeling uncomfortably full.
- Eating large amounts of food even when they aren't hungry.
- Eating alone due to embarrassment over how much they are eating.
- Feeling disgusted with themselves because they overeat.

Binge-eaters do not use purging behaviors to rid their bodies of calories, so they may be overweight for their age and height.

If you think your mentee may have an eating disorder, *she needs to get professional help.* Treatment usually includes working with a therapist on body image, self-esteem problems, and possible mood disorders; a dietician on healthy eating habits; and a doctor who monitors her weight gain, body functioning, and prescribed medications.

How You Can Be Supportive

If your mentee has an eating disorder, you can be supportive of her journey towards better health by doing the following:
1. Share your concerns with your mentee and her family if you think she may have an eating disorder. Be honest and nonjudgmental.
2. Help her family find the professional help your mentee needs to get better.
3. Avoid talking about food when you are eating together. Talk about other, more enjoyable subjects.
4. Avoid being overly watchful of your mentee's eating habits, food amounts, and food choices.
5. Cook together and try new healthy recipes.
6. Help her to develop other interests such as art classes or volunteer work to get her mind off her obsession with eating.
7. Avoid comments about his physical appearance or body shape, such as "You look better since you gained more weight."
8. Comment instead on his overall health. Use supportive statements such as "You look well rested," or "You seem to have a lot of energy today."
9. Let your mentee know that you care about her no matter how she looks.

Eating Disorder Information Resources

- Center for Eating Disorders. http://www.eating-disorders.com
- National Eating Disorders Association. http://www.nationaleatingdisorders.org
- ANRED: Anorexia Nervosa and Related Eating Disorders. http://www.anred.com
- Overeaters Anonymous. http://www.overeatersanonymous.org

Depression

Teenagers sometimes get the "blues" for a short period of time. Depression is not a temporary sad feeling. Depression is a serious health disorder caused by a combination of factors, including genetics, environment, medical conditions, substance abuse, hormonal changes, life events, and thought patterns that affect how a person reacts to events. If your mentee has five or more of the following symptoms over a two-week period, chances are he is clinically depressed.

Symptoms of Depression

- Depressed mood or sadness most of the time
- Restless and more irritable
- Lack of energy and feeling tired all of the time
- Inability to enjoy things that used to bring pleasure
- Withdrawal from friends and family
- Irritability, anger, or anxiety
- Inability to concentrate
- Unable to make decisions
- Significant weight loss or gain
- Significant change in sleep patterns
- Feelings of guilt and worthlessness
- Feelings of hopelessness and helplessness
- Headaches, stomachaches, backaches
- Aches and pains when nothing is physically wrong
- Pessimism and indifference
- Thoughts of death or suicide

Depression can affect people of any race, ethnic, or economic group. People who are clinically depressed need professional treatment. Depression can be treated through counseling and medical help. A therapist can help you talk through problems, improve your self-esteem, and learn better coping and problem solving skills. A physician can prescribe medications that can help relieve the symptoms of depression. Many people use a combination of therapy and medication to help them recover from depression.

If you think your mentee is depressed, share your concerns with her and her family. Assist them in getting your mentee the help she needs to recover.

Suicide

The Center for Disease Control and Prevention reports that *suicide is the third leading cause of death among teenagers.* The National Institute of Mental Health reports that about 60 percent of people who commit suicide have had a mood disorder, and *younger persons who kill themselves often have a substance abuse disorder in addition to being depressed.*

Warning Signs of Suicidal Thoughts

Although it is impossible to predict when a person is serious about taking his or her life, the following list provides warning signs to watch for:

- Pulling away from friends or family and losing the desire to go out
- Trouble concentrating or thinking clearly
- Changes in eating and sleeping habits
- Major changes in appearance that indicate they aren't taking care of themselves
- Talk about feeling hopeless or feeling guilty
- Talk about suicide
- Talk about death
- Talk about "going away"
- Self-destructive behavior such as alcohol and drug abuse or driving too fast
- No desire to take part in favorite activities
- Giving away of favorite possessions
- Having an actual plan to kill themselves
- Suddenly becoming very happy and cheerful after being depressed or sad for a long period of time

If your mentee exhibits any of these warning signs, you need to intervene immediately. He needs professional help and treatment. Experts in suicide prevention recommend the following approaches.

Suicide Prevention and Intervention Strategies

- If a person has any of the warning signs, ask her directly if she is considering suicide. Ask her if she has made a specific plan. Tell her that you care deeply about her and that help is available.
- Talking with a person who may be considering suicide may help him feel less alone and isolated, more cared about and understood. Your intervention may give him hope that there is another solution to his problems.
- If a person talks about committing suicide, take him seriously; listen non-judgmentally; and assist him in getting professional help.

- If you feel a person is in immediate danger of harming herself, do not leave her alone. Get her emergency help by calling 911.
- If you feel your mentee is in immediate danger of harming himself, limit his access to guns and other weapons.
- Get more information on suicide prevention from the National Strategy for Suicide Prevention at www.mentalhealth.org/suicideprevention.

The Suicide Helpline is 1-800-SUICIDE.

C. SAFETY

Learning how to keep yourself safe is an important life skill. This section summarizes safety tips you can share with your mentee to help him learn how to take care of himself at home, on the street, in the car, and on the Internet.

Safety At Home

1. Keep your doors locked even when you are home or plan to be gone only a few minutes.
2. Install a sturdy deadbolt lock on every outside door.
3. Have strong locks on all the windows.
4. Use a wooden rod to keep sliding glass doors closed.
5. Always close and lock garage doors before you drive away.
6. Do not leave your house key in the door lock, on a table by the front door, or hidden under a planter or over a door jam.
7. When moving to a new house or apartment, be sure that new locks are installed on the outside doors.
8. Keep the outside lights on after dark.
9. Clearly display your house number so emergency vehicles can easily locate your home.
10. Never open the door without looking outside through a peephole or window to be sure you know the person or persons.
11. If a stranger wants to come in to use the phone, do not let them. Offer instead to call for emergency assistance.
12. If a window or door has been forced open or broken while you were gone, do not enter or call out. Instead call 911 and wait for help to arrive.
13. Keep emergency phone numbers and the numbers where family members can be reached by every phone in the house.
14. Never let callers know you are home alone. Tell them your parents cannot come to the phone right now but will call them back later.

Safety on the Street

1. Always be alert to your surroundings and the people around you.
2. Walk confidently and at a steady pace.
3. Make eye contact with people when walking.
4. Whenever possible, walk with a friend.
5. Stay in well-lit areas. Avoid doorways, bushes, and alleys where someone might be hiding.
6. Do not respond to conversation from strangers; keep on walking.
7. Stand a safe distance away from a car that stops so the driver can talk to you.

Safety In The Car

1. Always wear a seat belt when riding in a car.
2. Do not drink and drive or ride in a car with a driver who has been drinking or using drugs.
3. If you're the driver, pay attention to your driving. If you're a passenger, do not distract the driver.
4. Lock all the car doors when entering or leaving the car.
5. Check inside the car to be sure no one is in the front or back seat before you get in.
6. Park in well lit areas.
7. Have your car keys in your hand, ready to open and get in the car quickly.
8. If you think someone is following you, drive to a well-lit area where there are people.
9. If your car breaks down, lift the hood, get back in the car, and lock the doors. When someone stops to check, ask the person to call for help.
10. Don't stop to help broken down motorists. Phone 911 for assistance.
11. When someone drives you home, ask the person to wait until you are safely inside.
12. If an emergency vehicle (i.e., police car or ambulance) stops you and you do not feel safe getting out of your car, use your cell phone to call 911 and ask them to verify that this is a valid stop. If you don't have a cell phone, turn on your emergency flashing lights and drive slowly to the nearest police station or public place before stopping.

Safety Riding Your Bicycle

1. Wear a bike helmet; *75% of all bicycle accidents involve an injury to the head.*
2. Be sure your bike helmet fits properly. The helmet should sit firmly on top of your head and not be tilted forward, backward, or to the side. The chinstrap should be pulled tight enough so that the helmet does not move around on your head.
3. Check to be sure the brakes and gears are working properly before you get on the bike.
4. Wear light and bright-colored, fluorescent clothes so that motorists can easily see you.
5. Put a rubber band or clip around your pants legs to be sure they don't get caught in the tire spokes.
6. Wear sturdy shoes. Don't wear cleats, high heels, flip-flops, or go barefoot.
7. Learn driving rules. Obey the laws.
8. Always ride on the right side of the road, in the same direction as the car traffic.
9. Use bike lanes or bike paths whenever available.
10. Always check for traffic in both directions, especially at intersections.
11. Don't ride too closely to parked cars to avoid doors being suddenly opened into you.
12. Use hand signals when changing lanes or turning.
13. If you have to ride at night, be sure to have reflectors and a light on your bike.
14. Don't wear headphones while biking; you need to hear what's going on around you.

Safety Using the Internet

1. When you are on any type of Internet public forum such as a chat room or blog, do not give out your full name, mailing address, telephone number, name of your school, credit card numbers, or any other information that could help someone determine your actual identity.
2. Use an on-line name that does not provide information about you.
3. Do not give out identifying information about your family or friends.
4. If someone you've met on the Internet wants to meet you in person, discuss it with your parents, and take a parent with you to the meeting. Suggest that the other person also bring his or her parent. Always meet in a public place like a restaurant or mall. Never go alone.
5. Do not respond to e-mail, chat comments, instant messages, or other messages that are hostile, belligerent, inappropriate, or in any way make you feel uncomfortable. Show these messages to a trusted adult. Then delete them.
6. Avoid chat rooms or discussion areas that look dangerous or provocative. Use chat rooms that have a chat moderator that supervises what is being said and will kick someone out of the chat room if they are inappropriate.
7. Have an updated version of virus protection software installed on your computer.
8. Do not download anything from your email or a website that you think may contain a virus.
9. Do not tell your password to anyone.
10. Remember, you cannot believe everything you read or that others tell you just because you found the information on an Internet website or chat room.

Safety On Dates

1. Consider double dating or going out with a group of friends the first few times you go out with a new person.
2. Know what the exact plans are for the date. Tell your parents about these plans, where you are going, contact information, and when you will be home. If your plans change, call and let your parents know.
3. Avoid using drugs or alcohol because you may make poor decisions about your safety while under the influence of these substances.
4. Do not be alone with someone who has been drinking or taking drugs. They may act differently and inappropriately when under the influence.
5. Do not get into a car with someone who has been drinking or using drugs.
6. Always get your own drink. Never put your drink down or leave it unsupervised. If you lose track of your drink, throw it out and get a fresh drink.
7. Do not leave the party or go anywhere with someone you do not know well.
8. Make sure you tell someone when you are leaving and with whom you are leaving.
9. Ask a friend to call you once you have had enough time to get home to be sure you arrived safely.
10. If you feel the situation is becoming dangerous, find a way to remove yourself safely.

11. Always take a cell phone or money/calling card to use a phone in case you need to call your parents, friends, or police for assistance.

First Aid / CPR Classes

Consider taking a first aid / CPR class with your mentee. Call your local chapter of the American Red Cross or the local hospital to find out when classes are offered.

Calling 911

1. Call 911 only for emergencies such as reporting a crime, a life-threatening event, need for medical assistance, an accident, or a fire.
2. Try to remain calm and speak slowly when you are talking to the 911 operator.
3. Be specific when providing the 911 operator with information:
   What is your name?
   What is the emergency?
   What happened?
   Where are you? (street address, mile marker, road signs)
   Who needs help?
   Who is with you?

4. Follow all directions that the 911 operator gives you.
5. Do not hang up the phone until the 911 operator says you can.
6. If you call 911 by accident, stay on the line. The 911 operator needs to make sure everything is okay. If you hang up before the operator says it is all right, the police may come to your location.
7. If you are using a cell phone, give the operator your phone number in case you are disconnected and she needs to call you back.
8. If you are in doubt about whether the situation is an emergency, call 911. The operator will decide if it's a real emergency.

Practice scenarios where you have your mentee make a pretend 911 call. If your mentee is an English language learner, this exercise is very important.

Teens and Safety Websites
- Online Safety for Kids & Teens. www.wiredteens.org
- Child Safety—National Crime Prevention Coalition. www.ncpc.org
- Staying Safe. www.kidshealth.org/teensafety/
- Safety First. www.safety1st.org
- Project Pave: Teens: Safety Planning Resources and Tips. www.project.pave.org

D. RELATIONSHIPS

Adolescence is usually a stormy time, with lots of ups and downs, as youth experiment with relationships. A teenage girl may hate her best friend in the morning, and they'll be back to being the best of friends by noon. A young man may sit nervously by the phone for hours while he builds up the courage to ask someone out on his first date. A girl may say, "He's my boy friend; we're going out together," even though they have never been on a date. A young person may break out in tears because his girl friend broke up with him.

If you have worked on building trust and open communications with your mentee, he will likely ask you for advice about his relationships with family, friends, and his romantic significant other. He may feel more comfortable confiding in you because you are not his parent, yet you have adult wisdom he won't find in his friends. Use the information in this section to help you answer his questions and provide him with guidance.

Healthy Relationships

Whether between parent and child, two friends, boy friend and girl friend, or mentor and mentee, you are in a healthy relationship if:

- You feel good about yourself when you are together.
- You enjoy and have fun doing activities together.
- You can relax and just be yourself when you are with this person.
- You talk and listen to each other attentively.
- You support each other.
- The relationship has a give and take balance, meaning you're not always the giver or always the taker.
- You respect and trust each other.
- You are honest with each other.
- You feel safe with the other person.
- You can talk through your disagreements without damaging the relationship.
- The other person does not pressure you to do anything you don't want to do or aren't comfortable doing.

Unhealthy Relationships

Your mentee may be in an unhealthy or even dangerous relationship if the other person does any of the following:

- Is very possessive. Gets angry when you spend time with or talk to your friends or someone of the opposite sex.
- Bosses you around; makes all the decisions. Your opinion doesn't seem to matter.
- Tells you what to wear, how to sit, what to eat, how to style your hair, etc.
- Gets in fights and loses his (her) temper a lot.
- Pressures you to do something you don't want to do; i.e., staying out after curfew, drinking, drugs, sex.
- Swears at you and calls you bad names.
- Blames you for his or her problems. It's always your fault, never their fault.
- Insults and embarrasses you in private and in front of other people.
- Hurts you physically.
- Steals from you.
- Gossips about you with others. Tells lies about you.
- Makes you feel scared of how he (she) will react.
- Always wants to know where you're at and with whom; calls to check up on you all the time.

If your mentee is in a relationship with someone who behaves like the person described above, initiate a discussion with him about how to establish healthy boundaries.

Establishing Healthy Boundaries

Establishing boundaries is how we protect and take care of ourselves. Your mentee needs to learn how to establish boundaries that will keep her out of unhealthy relationships. Envision yourself in a sphere. Inside the sphere is your personal space where you get to be safe, feel secure, and be respected. This sphere defines your boundaries. When someone does anything that intrudes upon your personal space and makes you feel scared, hurt, insulted, or taken advantage of, they have violated your boundaries.

Help your mentee learn and practice the following steps to establish and maintain healthy boundaries:

1. *Reinforce Positive Self-Concept*: Using the information and activities in Unit Two: Self-Concept and Life Success, help your mentee realize that he is a person who deserves to be treated with respect. He can use positive self-talk and affirmations to remind himself that he will not let others treat him poorly.

2. *Be Clear About Your Values*: Make a list with your mentee that describes how she would like others to treat her. Use the "Healthy Relationships" descriptors to begin your discussion. Some items on her list might be: "Don't yell at me; don't call me bad names; don't steal from me." The list provides her with a concrete visual border for her boundaries.

3.   *Overcome the Fear of Rejection*: Your mentee may be afraid to set boundaries with other people for fear they will leave or reject her. Teens are very concerned about fitting in with a certain group of friends. Your mentee may conform and do things she is not comfortable doing in order to be accepted by her clique. She may remain in an unhealthy relationship for fear of losing her boy friend. Have discussions with your mentee about the differences between healthy and unhealthy relationships. Have her write out the benefits vs. damages to her personally when she lets others violate her personal boundaries.

4.   *Practice Assertive Communication Skills*: When someone has violated your personal boundaries, a normal reaction is to feel angry or scared, or just plain sick to your stomach. When your emotions are high, you may move into a passive or aggressive communication style that will prevent you from getting your needs met. Review "Using Effective Speaking Styles" in Unit Three with your mentee. Have him practice using assertive communication when he's with you.

5.   *Add Consequences to "I-Messages"*: "I-Messages" were described in Unit Three: Communication Skills. The steps to giving boundary-setting "I-Messages" are:

   A. Describe specifically the behavior you dislike:

      When you raise your voice and swear at me...
      When you took my CD without my permission...
      When you gossip about me with your friends...

   B. Describe how the behavior makes you feel:

      I feel frightened and disrespected; I feel like you might hit me.
      I feel angry; I feel I cannot trust you to be alone with my things.
      I feel hurt and saddened; I feel that you don't value our friendship.

   C. Describe what you will do if it happens again (consequences):

      If you yell and swear at me again, I will hang up the phone (or walk away).
      If you take anything else from my room without my permission, you won't be allowed in my room.
      If you continue to gossip about me, we may not be able to be friends anymore.

6.   *Enforce the Consequences*: If the person continues to violate your boundaries, you must be willing to follow through with the consequences. Be sure that you choose consequences that you can live with if you have to enforce them.

7. *Practice Boundary Setting*: When your mentee feels that someone has violated his boundaries, help him put into words and practice with you what he will say to the violator.

Sexual Harassment

The Equal Employment Opportunity Commission (EEOC) provides this legal definition of sexual harassment:

Sexual harassment is any unwelcome sexual advances, requests for sexual favors, and other verbal or physical conduct of a sexual nature when:

1. Submission to such conduct is made either explicitly or implicitly as a term or condition of an individual's employment.
2. Submission to, or rejection of, such conduct by an individual is used as the basis for employment decisions affecting such individual.
3. Such conduct has the purpose or effect of unreasonably interfering with an individual's work performance or creating an intimidating, hostile, or offensive work environment.

Sexual harassment interferes with a student's right to learn, study, work, or participate in school activities and with an employee's ability to perform productively in a comfortable, supportive, and respectful environment. If your mentee feels she is being sexually harassed in school or at work, ask her to answer the questions taken from *"Sexual Harassment in Schools: It's No Laughing Matter"* developed by the Maryland Department of Education:

- Is the behavior of a sexual nature?
- Is the behavior unwelcome by anyone involved?
- Does the behavior make you or any other person feel uncomfortable?
- Does the behavior interfere with anyone's ability to learn or to enjoy school or classroom activities (or perform at work)?
- Does the behavior involve one person trying to have some kind of power over another person?
- Is the behavior part of a pattern of repeated behavior?
- Would you want this behavior directed toward a member of your family or toward a friend?

Examples of sexual harassment behaviors include but are not limited to requests for sexual favors, lewd comments, sexual name calling, dirty jokes, unwanted touching, cornering, leering, spreading sexual rumors, suggestive gestures, obscene T-shirts, hats, pins, or graffiti, catcalls, howling, and sexual assault.

If your mentee is being sexually harassed at school or at work, have him implement the following steps:

1. Do not ignore the behavior.
2. Use a boundary-setting "I-message" to tell the harasser that his/her behavior is unwelcome and offensive.
3. Deliver the boundary-setting message publicly in front of others.
4. Document the behavior and your responses using the *Sexual Harassment Report* form.
5. Talk to your parents and others who may also be victims of the harasser. Support each other and work to get the harassing behavior to stop.
6. File a verbal and then a written complaint with the principal or work supervisor.
7. If the principal or supervisor takes no action, take your complaint to their supervisor.
8. If the sexual harassment continues and no one in authority will take action, consider filing a complaint with the Office of Civil Rights.

Sexual Harassment Report

Your Name:

Date of Incident:

Time of Incident:

Location of Incident:

Name of Harasser(s):

Names of Witnesses:

Description of What Happened:

How did the behavior make you feel?

What did you do in response to the behavior?

Who did you report the incident to? When did you report it?

What did the person you reported the incident to do?

Conflict Resolution

Adolescents will at times tease, accuse, shove, or steal from each other. Disagreements are common. A major concern is that conflict among teenagers can result in violence. They don't want to lose face or be considered weak because they refuse to fight. Or they lose their tempers, and the fists start to fly. Many schools now have peer mediation or counseling programs that help young people resolve their differences. If your mentee asks you for help in resolving a conflict she has with another person, follow the guidelines below that were developed by the National Youth Violence Prevention Resource Center.

1. Get the people involved to agree to work out a peaceful solution to the conflict.
2. Establish the ground rules; i.e., no name-calling, no yelling, listening respectfully, waiting until it is your turn to talk.
3. Get everyone's perspective—his or her versions of what happened. Write down what is said and ask everyone to listen to each other without judging or blaming. Using I-messages will be helpful here.
4. List the points that everyone agrees with.
5. Ask each party what they feel they need to have happen in order to resolve the conflict.
6. Have each person brainstorm alternative solutions where all parties involved will get at least some of their needs met.
7. Have the parties involved discuss the suggested solutions and how they feel about each one. Ask them to negotiate and suggest possible compromises.
8. Create an agreement as to how they will resolve their conflict. Write it down and have all parties sign off.

Check back later to see how the conflict resolution agreement is going. Ask your mentee what he learned from the process.

Prejudice and Discrimination

Name-calling, hateful graffiti, and put-downs are common occurrences in middle schools and high schools. Youth learn biases, stereotypes, and prejudices from home, their music, movies, television, and even in class. Your role as mentor includes challenging your mentee's stereotypes and prejudices that are having a negative effect on his life and those around him.

Discuss with your mentee the definitions of the terms below:

Stereotype: An oversimplified, non-scientific, judgmental generalization about a person or group of people without regard for individual differences.

Prejudice: A pre-judgment, attitude or learned belief about a person or group of people without sufficient knowledge. Often based on stereotypes.

Discrimination: Oppressive actions and behaviors. A denial of justice and fair treatment by individuals and institutions.

Continue your discussion by asking your mentee to share with you what stereotypes and prejudices he may have. Then ask him these questions:

- Where did you learn these stereotyped labels, prejudices, and discriminatory behaviors?
- Who do you know from this cultural group that does not fit the negative stereotypes you have?
- How do you think these labels, beliefs, and behaviors affect you?
- How do these labels, beliefs, and behaviors affect others?
- What advantages will you experience by eliminating these stereotypes, prejudices, and discriminatory behaviors from your life?
- What can you do to help yourself eliminate these negative stereotypes, prejudices, and behaviors from your life?

Use the following strategies to help your mentee begin eliminating her stereotyped thinking and prejudices:

1. Be mindful of your language; avoid making stereotypical remarks and challenge those made by others.
2. Challenge those who tell jokes that are offensive and put-down others.
3. Learn more about other cultures through books and movies written by people from those cultures.
4. Attend cultural events such as Cinco de Mayo, Juneteenth, and Pow Wows.
5. Visit museums and art galleries that specialize in a specific cultural base.
6. Introduce your mentee to your friends who are from a different culture.
7. Volunteer together for projects that will provide an opportunity for your mentee to work with youth and adults from different cultural backgrounds.

Helpful Websites on Educating Youth About Prejudice and Discrimination:

- Southern Poverty Law Center: Tolerance.org
- American-Arab Anti-Discrimination Committee: www.adc.org
- National Association for the Advance of Colored People: www.naacp.org
- American Jewish Committee: www.ajc.org
- Gay Lesbian Straight Education Network: www.glsen.org
- Anti-Defamation League: www.adl.org
- Educators for Social Responsibility: www.esrnational.org
- Facing History and Ourselves: www.facinghistory.org

As our country's population becomes increasingly more diverse and as communication and transportation technology bring us in closer contact with cultures from around the world, your mentee will need to continually examine his beliefs and work on eliminating his stereotypes, prejudices, and discriminatory behaviors, if he is to be successful in life.

E. DECISION-MAKING

Teenagers must make decisions every day that affect their lives in all five areas of growth described in Unit One.

Intellectual Decisions:	How to organize their work and time. Which classes to take.
Moral Decisions:	To cheat or not to cheat on a test. To join in or put a stop to harassment.
Emotional Decisions:	How to manage anger. How to express affection appropriately.
Physical Decisions:	What to eat to stay healthy. How to say "No" to drugs and alcohol.
Social Decisions:	How to handle negative peer pressure. How to choose positive friends.

As a mentor, you can help your mentee learn and practice decision-making skills by:

- Modeling good decision-making. When your mentee is with you, talk aloud through the process you use as you make decisions.
- Provide your mentee with opportunities to make decisions that are age-appropriate. Help by talking her through the steps to decision-making.
- Respect his decisions and allow him to live with the consequences—both good and bad.
- Help her evaluate the results of her decision. Help her learn from decisions that have a negative outcome.
- Help your mentee learn from others' decisions by using movies, TV shows, books, and the experiences of friends and family. What decision had to be made? What did the person decide? What was the outcome? What would your mentee have done? How could the outcome have changed if the person had made a different decision?

Steps to Decision-Making

Decision-making is a skill that must be actively taught to youth. Teens need to learn and practice good decision-making skills so they are able to make the hard decisions that come from negative peer pressure. The steps to decision-making are:

Scenario: *Maria's friend wants her to take basic math next year so they can be in the same class. Maria needs Algebra to get into college.*

I. **Recognize the opportunity to make a decision.** Sometimes young people don't realize they have a choice to make. If your mentee tells you about a difficult situation he's facing, tell him, "It sounds like you have an important decision to make."

Maria has to decide whether to take basic math to please her friend or take algebra to prepare for college.

2. **Ask yourself, "Whose decision is this?"** Teens get caught up in each other's lives and events, and personal boundaries get entangled. Help your mentee think through whose decision it is.

Maria's friend may pressure her to take basic math so they can hang together in class. However, the decision is Maria's to make. It is her life that will be affected in the long term.

3. **Gather more information.** Once your mentee realizes he has a decision to make, ask him if he has enough information to make a wise choice. What additional information would be helpful? How can he access this information?

Maria's choices are to take basic math or algebra. Are there more options? Could Maria encourage her friend to take algebra with her? Are there other classes they could take together?

4. **Brainstorm and analyze options for action.** Your mentee needs to come up with options and decide the pros and cons of each possible choice.

Option:	Takes basic math.
Pros:	Pleases her friend.
Cons:	Misses out on math needed for college.

Option:	Takes algebra.
Pros:	Takes math needed for college.
Cons:	Disappoints friend.

Option:	Talks friend into taking algebra with her.
Pros:	Both take math needed for college.
Cons:	None.

Option:	Takes algebra and a different class with her friend.
Pros:	Pleases her friend and takes math needed for college.
Cons:	None.

5. **Make the decision and follow through.** Your mentee will need to choose one of the options.

   Maria talks her friend into taking algebra with her.

6. **Monitor and evaluate the results of the decision.** Check back with your mentee to help her evaluate the results of her decision. If the results are positive, congratulate her on a wise choice. If things are not going well as a result of her decision, ask her what she has learned and what she might do differently the next time a similar situation arises.

Use these Steps to Decision-Making to help your mentee work through the process when he has important decisions to make.

G. CIVIC RESPONSIBILITY

A Child Trends Research Brief, *"Encouraging Civic Engagement: How Teens Are (or Are Not) Becoming Responsible Citizens"* reported that:

- Only 32% of 18 to 24-year olds voted in the 2000 Presidential elections.
- Only 30 to 50% of the country's teenagers participated in community service activities.
- Only 14% of 15 to 24-year-olds took part in an organization dealing directly with politics or government.

In a democracy such as ours, where the majority of citizens who vote rule by electing officials who represent their interests and beliefs, it is vitally important to encourage young people to get involved in civic activities.

Child Trends reviewed 60 studies of civic engagement of youth. Their findings provide the following activities you can do with your mentee to help develop his sense of civic responsibility.

- Teach your mentee about the election process and government systems that exist in your community.
- Study the election issues and community concerns together. Read the local papers, attend city council and legislative sessions, and sit in on hearings that allow for community input on issues to be on the next election ballot.
- Take your mentee with you when you go to vote. If he is 18 years old, be sure he is registered to vote so he can vote when you do.
- Help your mentee decide which candidates support her point-of-view and interests. Suggest she get involved in the candidate's campaign.
- Seek out community projects where you and your mentee can volunteer.
- Provide your mentee with positive praise and encouragement for his involvement in civic activities.
- Check out the America's Promise: The Alliance for Youth website for more ideas. www.americaspromise.org.

H. GOAL SETTING

The Importance of Setting Goals

Explain to your mentee the importance of setting goals. Emphasize that goals will:

- Help her plan for her future and realize her dreams.
- Guide his decision-making.
- Provide her with the motivation to persist when the 'going gets tough.'
- Help him focus his time, energy, and resources.
- Help her determine and set priorities.
- Improve his performance at school and work.
- Increase her pride and satisfaction in her achievements.
- Improve his self-esteem and self-confidence when goals are achieved.

Steps to Setting Goals

1. **Develop a long-term goal.** Long-term goals will take several weeks, months, or perhaps even the entire school year to accomplish. The goal must be realistic and reachable, action-oriented, measurable, and stated in a positive way.

   I will improve my social studies grade from a "D" to a "B" by the next report card.

2. **Develop short-term goal steps to help you achieve your long-term goal.** Short-term goals can be accomplished within a couple of weeks or a month and contribute to helping you reach your long-term goal.

   I will listen in class and take good notes. I will do all of my homework assignments. I will study for the tests.

3. **Identify your support system and motivation.** Who and what can help you achieve your short and long term goals?

   Support: *My mom will help me with my homework; my best friend is in the same class and will study with me for the tests.*

   Motivation: *When I have brought my grade up to a "B," my mom said she'd buy me new shoes, or I could invite my friends for a sleepover.*

4. **Identify the obstacles and how you will overcome them**. Who and what may make it difficult or prevent you from reaching your goal?

Obstacles: *I don't like the teacher, so I don't pay attention in class.*

Overcome by: *Tape my goal statement on the front cover of my notebook to remind me that I need to listen and take good notes. Compare my notes with my best friend's after each class.*

5. **Develop a weekly checklist to monitor the goal steps**. Check off the short-term goal steps you accomplish each week. This will give you a sense of accomplishment and help you stay focused on the long-term goal.

Week One: *Took good notes in class.*
Goal List: *Did my homework every night. Studied for the test.*

6. **Evaluate your progress and goal attainment**. Did you achieve your goal within the timeframe you set for yourself? If not, list the reasons you feel you were not successful. Make adjustments and set a new goal for yourself.

I only got a "C" in social studies on my report card. I know that I did not study long enough for two of the tests. I put off studying until the night before and that did not give me enough time. I did improve my grade, and I feel good about that, but I still want to get a "B".

7. **Set a new goal.**

My new goal is to study two or three evenings every week for the test so that I can bring my grade up to a "B" on the next report card.

Goal Attainment Hints

- Have your mentee write her long and short-term goal statements on several 3"x 5" cards. Ask her to tape a card in places she will see them throughout the day to remind her of her goals: bathroom mirror, school locker, class notebook, etc.
- Tell him not to share his goal with anyone who may tease him or discount what he is trying to accomplish. Negative attitudes of family and friends will only get in the way and drag him down. Instead, tell him to use plenty of positive self-talk to motivate him towards achieving his goals.
- Remind your mentee to consider her goals when she makes decisions throughout the week. Will her choices support and help her achieve her goals or will they become obstacles?

- Suggest that your mentee develop goals for each of the five areas of growth: intellectual, physical, social, emotional, and moral.
- Help your mentee monitor goal attainment progress by checking with her each week on what she has accomplished, what new obstacles she has encountered, and how she plans to overcome the obstacles.
- Provide positive, encouraging support to your mentee as he works towards his goals. Plan a special celebration to reward him when he has successfully reached his goals.

A person without goals is like a boat without a rudder—
he has no control over his destiny.
He just drifts along and goes wherever the tide takes him.
He starts each day without direction and purpose in his life.

UNIT FIVE: BIBLIOGRAPHY

4 Girls Health. "Drugs, Alcohol & Smoking– Straight Talk." http://www.4girls.gov/substance/tobacco.htm. (accessed 5/9/05)

4 Girls Health. "Mind—Emotion Commotion." http://www.4girls.gov/mind/stress.htm. (accessed 5/10/05)

4 Girls Health. "Relationships—Friends and Family." http://www.4girls.gov/relationships/healthy_relationships.htm. (accessed 5/10/05)

ACADV—Academy of Domestic Violence. "Dating Violence." http://www.acadv.org/dating.html. (accessed 7/14/05)

"All About Depression." http://www.allaboutdepression.com

American Academy of Family Physicians. "Talking to Your Child About STDs." http://www.kidshealth.org

American Academy of Child & Adolescent Psychiatry. "Teens: Alcohol and Other Drugs." http://www.aacap.org/publications/factsfam/teendrug.htm. (accessed 7/14/05)

American Lung Association. "Smoking and Teens Fact Sheet." http://www.lungusa.org/site/pp.asp?c=dvLUK900E&b=39871. (accessed 7/14/05)

America's Promise: The Alliance for Youth website. www.americaspromise.org (accessed 8/6/05)

Anderson, Kare. "Fourteen Winning Strategies for Handling Conflict." Effective Communication Skills. Http://www.hodu.com/negotiation-skills.html. (accessed 6/15/05)

Anti-Defamation League. (2001). *101 Ways to Combat Prejudice.* New York, NY: Anti-Defamation League.

Burke, Ray and Herron, Ron. (1996). *Common Sense Parenting.* Boys Town, NE: The Boys Town Press.

Burney, Robert. "Setting Personal Boundaries—Protecting Self." Joy2MeU website. http://www.joy2meu.com/Personal_Boundaries.htm (accessed 8/2/05)

Center for Young Women's Health: Children's Hospital Boston. "Healthy Eating for Teens: Balancing Good Nutrition and Fun." http://www.youngwomenshealth.org/healthyeating.html. (accessed 5/9/05)

Center for Young Women's Health: Children's Hospital Boston. "Information About Eating Disorders." http://www.youngwomenshealth.org/eating_disorders.html. (accessed 5/9/05)

Center for Young Women's Health: Children's Hospital Boston. "Supporting Teens with Eating Disorders: A Guide for Family Members & Close Friends." http://www.youngwomenshealth.org/supportteens.html. (accessed 5/9/05)

Center for Young Women's Health: Children's Hospital Boston. "Safety on the Internet: A Guide for Teens." http://www.youngwomenshealth.org/safety_on_the_net.html. (accessed 5/9/05)

Center for Young Women's Health: Children's Hospital Boston. "Safety on the Streets Guide." http://www.youngwomenshealth.org/safety_on_the_streets.html. (accessed 5/9/05)

Center for Young Women's Health. "Healthy Relationships." www.youngwomenshealth.org/teensafe.html. (accessed 7/14/05)

Center for Young Women's Health: Children's Hospital Boston. "Healthy Relationships: A Guide for Teenagers." http://www.youngwomenshealth.org/healthy_relat.html. (accessed 5/9/05)

Center for Young Women's Health: Children's Hospital Boston. "Safety in Relationships: A Guide for Teens." http://www.youngwomenshealth.org/safety_in_relat.html. (accessed 5/9/05)

Centers for Disease Control and Prevention. WISQARS (Web-based Injury Statistics Qury and Reporting System).

Cline, Foster and Fay, Jim. (1992). *Parenting Teens with Love and Logic.* Colorado Springs, CO: Pinon Press.

Colorado Coalition Against Sexual Assault. "Child Sexual Abuse—What Parents Need to Know." www.ccasa.org/documents/child_sexual-abuse-tips-for-parents.pdf. (accessed 3/7/05)

Community Resilience. "Stress Management for Teenagers." http://www.communityresilience.com/Information/StressManagementforTeensbrochure. htm. (accessed 7/14/05)

National Youth Violence Prevention Resource Center. "Conflict Resolution." http://www.safeyouth.org/scripts/teens/conflict.asp. (accessed 8/2/05)

Donohue, Gene. "Goal Setting—Powerful Written Goals in 7 Easy Steps!" Top Achievement. http://www.topachievement.com/goalsetting.html. (accessed 7/14/05)

Findingstone Counseling. "Helping Teenagers with Stress." http://www.findingstone. com/allkindsofstuff/stress/teenstress.htm. (accessed 7/14/05)

GetNetWise. "Safety Tips for Teens." http://kids.getnetwise.org/safetyguide/teens. (accessed 7/14/05)

Girls and Boys Town Website. "Peer Pressure . . ." http://www.girlsandboystown. org/hotline/KidTeenTips.asp (accessed 8/1/05)

Golden, Bernard. "Healthy Anger Management for Teens." New Living Magazine. http://www.newlving.com/issues/jan_2004/articles/anger%20management%20for%teen. (accessed 7/14/05)

HAC: Health Awareness Connection. "Young People's Guide to Sexually Transmitted Diseases (STDs) and AIDS/HIV Disease." http://www.healthac.org/stdguide.html. (accessed 7/14/05)

Harper, Gary. "Once upon a Conflict: The Journey from Confrontation to Collaboration." Effective Communication Skills. Http://www.hodu.com/conflict.shtml. (accessed 6/15/05)

Heacox, Diane. (1991). *Up From Underachievement.* Minneapolis, MN: Free Spirit Publishing Inc.

Health Pages. "STDs: AIDS Is Not The Only Threat." http://www.thehealthpages. com/articles/ar-stds.html. (accessed 7/14/05)

"Healthy Relationships." Advocates for Youth. http://www.advocatesforyouth.org/ youth/health/relationships/index.htm. (accessed 8/1/05)

Herron, Ron and Peter, Val. (1998). *What's Right for Me?* Boys Town, NE: The Boys Town Press.

Herron, Ron and Peter, Val. "Making Friends." Girls and Boys Town website. http://www.girlsandboystown.org/parents/tips/makingfriends.asp. (accessed 8/1/05)

Herron, Ron and Sorensen, Kathleen. (1998). *Unmasking Sexual Con Games: Parent Guide.* Boys Town, NE: The Boys Town Press.

Kaiser Family Foundation. (2000). "2000 National Survey of Teens on HIV/AIDS."

Kysilko, David and Murdock, Katheryn Wells. (1993,1998). *Sexual Harassment in Schools: What It Is, What to Do."* Alexandria, Virginia: National Association of State Boards of Education.

Larimer County Sheriff's Office. (2004) *Emergency Preparedness Guide.* Fort Collins, CO.

Magid, Larry. "E-Mail Etiquette, With Some Rules to Extinguish Flame-Throwing." http://www.safeteens.com/etiquette.htm. (accessed 7/14/05)

Meyer, Janet. (2000). "Rape Myths." http://www.ccasa.org/documents/Rape_Myths_&_Facts.pdf. (accessed 5/9/05)

Meyer, Janet. (2000). "Issues for Teachers in Sexual Violence Prevention Education." http://www.ccasa.org/documents/Issues_for_Teachers.pdf. (accessed 5/9/05)

Miller, Carol and VanDecar, Elena. (2004). *Parenting for Academic Success.* Denver, CO: Latin American Research and Service Agency.

Mind Tools. "Achieving Goals and Feedback." http://www.psychwww.com/mtsite/pgacgoal.html. (accessed 7/14/05)

My Goal Manager. "Requirements for Successful Goal Setting and Achievement." http://www.mygoalmanager.com/goals/goalTips.asp. (accessed 7/14/05)

National Youth Violence Prevention Resource Center. "Facts for Teens: Teen Suicide." www.safeyouth.org. (accessed 7/14/05)

The New Food Label. U.S. Food and Drug Administration. http://www.fda.gov/opacom/backgrounders/foodlabel/newlabel.html. (accessed 7/20/05)

NIMH—National Institute of Mental Health. "Let's Talk About Depression." http://www.nimh.nih.gov/publicat/letstalk.cfm. (accessed 7/15/05)

NIMH—National Institute of Mental Health. "What To Do When A Friend Is Depressed." http://www.nimh.nih.gov/publicat/friend. (accessed 7/15/05)

NIMH—National Institute of Mental Health. "Eating Disorders: Facts About Eating Disorders And The Search For Solutions." http://www.nimh.nih.gov/publicat/eating-disorders.cfm. (accessed 7/15/05)

NIMH—National Institute of Mental Health. "Frequently Asked Questions About Suicide." http://www.nimh.nih.gov/suicideprevention/suicidefaq.cfm. (accessed 7/15/05)

National Highway Traffic and Safety Administration. "10 Smart Routes to Bicycle Safety." http://www.nhtsa.dot.gov/people/injury/pedbimot/bike/10Smartroutesbicycle/index.htm (accessed 7/26/05)

National Highway Traffic and Safety Administration. "Safety Belts and Older Teens—2005 Report." http://www.nhtsa.dot.gov (accessed 7/26/05)

National Women's Health Resource Center, Inc. (2004). *Family Self-Care Handbook.*

National Sexual Violence Resource Center. "Materials on Sexual Violence in Spanish." http://www.nsvrc.org/saam_new/ (accessed 5/905)

NIDA for Teens—National Institute on Drug Abuse. "The Science Behind Drug Abuse." http://teens.drugabuse.gov/. (accessed 7/14/05)

Not-On-Tobacco. American Lung Association. "Q & A for Teens." http://www.lungusa.org/site/pp.aspx?c=dvLUK900E&b=39869&printmode=1. (accessed 7/14/05)

Parenting Teens. "Teen Depression." http://www.parentteen.com/teen_depression.html. (accessed 7/14/05)

Parenting Teens. "Helping Teens Handle Stress." http://www.parentteen.com/teen_stress.html. (accessed 7/14/05)

Payne, Lauren Murphy and Rohling, Claudia. (1997). *A Leader's Guide to We Can Get Along.* Minneapolis, MN: Free Spirit Publishing, Inc.

Potter-Efron, Ron and Potter-Efron, Pat. (1995). *Letting Go of Anger.* New York, NY: Barnes and Noble Books.

President's Council on Physical Fitness and Sports. "Physical Activity Fact Sheet." http://www.fitness.gov/resources_factsheet.htm. (accessed 7/14/05)

Ramsey, Lydia. "Etiquette for Meeting People in Business." http://www.hodu.com/meeting-etiquette.shtml. (accessed 6/15/05)

Riskystuff.com. "What is HIV and how do you get it?" "Key facts about STDs." http://www.riskystuff.com/aids.htm.

SAFETEENS.COM. "Basic Rules of Online Safety for Teens." http://www.safeteens.com/teenrules.htm. (accessed 7/14/05)

Sears, William and Sears, Martha. (2002). *The Successful Child: What Parents Can Do to Help Kids Turn Out Well.* Boston, MA: Little, Brown and Company.

Stevens, Joy. "Best Friends: How to Grow a Friend." http://www.cyberparent.com/friendship/growdirectory.htm. (accessed 8/1/05)

Strauss, Susan and Espeland, Pamela. (1992). *Sexual Harassment and Teens.* Minneapolis, MN: Free Spirit Press.

TeensHealth. "Alcohol." http://www.kidshealth.org/teen/drug_alcohol/alcohol/alcohol.html. (accessed 7/14/05)

TeensHealth. "Hygiene Basics." http://www.teenshealth.org/PageManager.jsp?dn=KidsHealth&lic=1&ps=207&cat_id=201. (accessed 7/14/05)

TeensHealth. "Depression." http://www.teenshealth.org/PageManager.jsp?dn+KidsHealth&lic_1&ps=207&cat_id=20123&art. (accessed 7/14/05)

TeensHealth. "My Friend Is Talking About Suicide. What Should I Do?" http://kidshealth.org/PageManager.jspdn+KidsHealth&lic=1&ps=207&cat_id=20128&art. (accessed 7/14/05)

TeensHealth. "Suicide." http://www.kidshealth.org/PageManager.jsp?dn=KidsHealth&lic=1&ps=207&cat_id=20123&art... (accessed 7/14/05)

TeensHealth. "How Can I Deal With My Anger?" http://www.kidshealth.org/teen/question/emotions/deal_with_anger.html. (accessed 7/14/05)

TeensHealth. "I Think My Friend May Have An Eating Disorder. What Should I Do?" http://www.kidshealth.org/teen/food_fitness/problems/friend_eating_disorder.html. (accessed 7/14/05)

TeensHealth. "Internet Safety: Safe Surfing Tips for Teens." http://www.kidshealth.org/teen/safety/safebasics/internet_safety.html. (accessed 7/14/05)

TeensHealth. "Dealing With An Emergency." http://www.kidshealth.org/teen/safety/safebasics/911.html. (accessed 7/14/05)

TeensHealth. "Bike Safety." http://www.kids.health.org/teen/safety/safebasics/bike_safety.html. (accessed 7/14/05)

Texas Department of State Health Services. "Addressing Bias—Promoting Understanding." http://www.dshs.state.tx.us/schoolhealth/bias.shtm. (accessed 7/14/05)

Time Thoughts. "Goal Setting: Why Should I Set Goals?" http://www.timethought.com/goalsetting/WhySetGoals. (accessed 7/14/05)

Tips for Teens. "The Truth about Tobacco." http://www.health.org/_usercontrols/printpage.aspx?FromPage=http%3A//www.health.org. (accessed 7/14/05)

USDA—United States Department of Agriculture. "Dietary Guidelines for Americans 2005." http://www.health.gov/dietaryguidelines/dga2005/document/html/brochure.htm. (accessed 7/14/05)

Welker, Eileene. "Decision Making/Problem Solving With Teens." Ohio State University Extension Factsheet. Http://ohioline.osu.edu/hyg-fact/5000/5301.html. (accessed 7/14/05)

"What to Do if You Are Being Sexually Harassed." Guilderland, NY: Guilderland Central School District. http://www.guilderlandschools.org/district/Job%20openings/sexualharassment2.htm. (accessed 8/2/05)

Wholistic Stress Control Institute. "Teen Stress." http://www.mindspring.com/~wholistic/teens_stress.html. (accessed 7/14/05)

Yager, Jan. "Building Friendships from Casual Friends." http://www.cyberparent.com/friendship/build.htm. (accessed 8/1/05)

Zaff, Jonathan. and Michelsen, Erik. (October, 2002). "Encouraging Civic Engagement: How Teens Are (or Are Not) Becoming Responsible Citizens." Child Trends Research Brief. Washington, DC. www.childtrends.org. (accessed 7/14/05)

UNIT SIX: AFTER HIGH SCHOOL -
Career Planning, Post-Secondary Education, and Employability Skills

A. Choosing a Career

Self-Assessment
Career Planning
Career Exploration

B. Post-Secondary Education

High School Portfolio
Post-Secondary Education Options
Selecting a Post-Secondary School
Campus Visits
School Application Process
Post-Secondary Expenses
Paying for Post-Secondary Education

C. Employability Skills

21st Century Job Skills
Developing a Resume
Cover Letter
References
Filling Out Job Applications
Job Interviewing

A. CHOOSING A CAREER

A 10th grade student I was tutoring told me she wanted to be a store manager someday. When I asked what she thought a store manager did, she didn't really know. I mentioned that one of the manager's tasks was to do most of the paperwork involved in running the store. Quite abruptly, she said, "Well, forget that, 'cause I hate doing paperwork."

When choosing a career path, the first step is to do a self-assessment to determine your likes, dislikes, strengths, and personal preferences that will influence the type of job you would enjoy. Then move into career planning and exploration to find jobs that would be a good match with your self-assessment results.

Self-Assessment

Help your mentee fill out the Self-Assessment Survey. He needs to spend time thinking about these questions before he begins his career planning and exploration. Be sure he fills in the date. The information he puts on his self-assessment today will change over the months and years ahead.

What activities do I enjoy doing? List the activities you do that are fun and enjoyable. Break the activity down into the specific parts that turn you on. For example, if you enjoy skateboarding, you might also list: being physically active, being outdoors, improving and mastering my skateboarding skills.

What activities do I dislike doing? List the types of activities you find boring and uncomfortable? Again, break the activity down into the specific parts you find distasteful. The 10th grader described above was clear that she didn't like to do paperwork. When asked why she didn't like doing paperwork, the student said she didn't like being stuck behind a desk. She wanted to be out in the store meeting and helping customers.

What are my hobbies? Hobbies are activities that bring you satisfaction. You work on hobbies during your free time when you aren't in school, doing homework, or working. Hobbies could include collecting items such as stamps and coins; playing sports; practicing and performing in a band or choir; doing arts and crafts, fishing, and so forth.

What are my favorite subjects in school? The subjects you most enjoy and do well in might influence your choice of careers. If you absolutely hate math, bookkeeping and accounting would not be good career choices for you. If you love science and biology, you might want to consider a career in the medical field.

What special skills or talents do I have? List your strength areas here. Do you speak a second language? Does computer know-how come easy for you? Do you work really well with children?

What are my personal characteristics or preferences? The personal preferences listed on the survey are only a few of the items that impact the jobs you might consider.

What types of jobs seem interesting to me now? Why? Even though your mentee will change jobs and career paths several times during his life, have him list jobs he thinks would be a good match for him today? Have him list the reasons these would be jobs he would enjoy. For example, he might list vet assistant or fish and game warden because he likes working with animals.

If you are working with your mentee over a long period of time, have her fill out the Self-Assessment Survey every six months to determine how her interests and skills have changed and what impact these changes may have on her career planning. Have your mentee use the survey to help her plan for a career where she will be able to do the things she enjoys, use her talents and skills, and work in an environment that suits her personal preferences.

An important part of life success is being able to do
what you love to do and get paid for it.

Self-Assessment Survey

Your Name_____ Date _____

What activities do I enjoy doing?

What activities do I dislike doing?

What are my favorite subjects in school?

What are my hobbies?

What special skills or talents do I have?

What are my personal characteristics or preferences?

_____	Work alone	_____	Work in groups
_____	Work with my hands	_____	Work on thinking tasks
_____	Work outside	_____	Work indoors
_____	Work 9 to 5 job	_____	Work flexible hours
_____	Work close to home	_____	Commute to work
_____	Work in big city	_____	Work in small town
_____	Like routine tasks	_____	Like variety in my work

What types of jobs seem interesting to me now? Why?

Career Planning

Adolescents are present-focused and don't usually think about how their choices and behaviors today will affect them in the future. Help your mentee visualize his preferred future lifestyle and the type of job he will need in order to earn enough money to support that lifestyle. This activity is a good first step in career planning.

Your Future Lifestyle

A 9th grade student was asked to prepare a budget for his life at age 18 years, living single with no kids, and a second budget for his life at age 28 years, married with two children. When he realized how much it would cost him to support two children, he said, "Forget it. I'm not having any kids."

Teenagers usually do not realize how expensive it is to be an independent adult; they have not stopped to think if their minimum wage job will provide them with enough income to pay their bills. Use the *Budgeting for Your Future Lifestyle* form to help your mentee figure out how much it will cost to live on her own. If your mentee does not know the cost of each budget item, have her ask her adult family members how much the items cost them each month.

After she gets monthly expense totals, have her figure out what she will earn each month at different jobs. For example:

- A fast food clerk earns $7 per hour, works 160 hours per month, and earns a monthly salary of $1,120.
- A secretary earns $10 per hour, works 160 hours per month, and earns a monthly salary of $1,600.
- A nurse earns $26 per hour, works 160 hours per month, and earns a monthly salary of $4,160.
- An engineer is a salaried position that pays $65,000 per year or $5,416 per month.

Now have your mentee multiply these salaries out for 1, 10, and 20 years to help him determine if the time and effort he spends now on preparing for a high-paying career is worth the return in salary earnings over his lifetime. For example:

- The fast food clerk's salary of $13,440 per year multiplied by 10 years comes out to $134,440, and multiplied by 20 years results in total earnings of $268,800.

This amount may seem like a lot of money to a teenager until he does the math with the engineer's job.

- The engineer's yearly salary of $65,000 multiplied by 10 years equals earnings of $650,000, and multiplied by 20 years results in total earnings of $1,300,000.

The budgeting and salary projection activities are usually a rude awakening for most teenagers. Help your mentee see that working hard in school today, going on to post-secondary education, and doing what he can now to prepare himself for a high-paying job is an investment in his future that pays a good return.

Budgeting for Your Future Lifestyle

Monthly Budget Items	Age 18, Single, No Kids	Age 28, Married, 2 Kids
Rent or House Payment		
Renter's or Home Owner's Insurance		
Utilities (electric, gas, water, sewer)		
Telephone		
Cable TV		
Car Payment		
Car Insurance		
Car Repairs/Gasoline		
Health Insurance/Medical Costs		
Food		
Clothes		
Entertainment		
Savings		
Miscellaneous Expenses		
Monthly Total		

Your Dream Job

Using the information on the *Self-Assessment Survey* as a guide, have your mentee describe the Dream Job she would like to have. Ask her to think about and respond to these questions:

- What amount of salary would she like to earn?
- Where geographically would he like to work? Big city? On the coast? In another country?
- Would she like to have her own business or work for a corporation?
- Would he like a job where he travels a lot?
- Does she want a 40-hour workweek or would she be willing to work longer hours to get the job done?
- Does an informal, casual-dress work environment appeal to him over a formal, suit-and-tie company?
- Does she want to work with people? Animals? Machines? Computers?
- Is there a particular field of work that sounds more interesting than others?

Tell your mentee that dreaming has no limits. Once he has an idea of what his Dream Job might look like, he can move into Career Exploration activities to find jobs that come close to his dream.

Career Assessments

Another method for helping your high school mentee do career planning is to have her take several career assessments. Her school counselor, the school's vocational teachers, or the local employment office will be able to give her one or more types of career assessments. Caution her that these assessments only provide her with guidance and ideas for careers she may not have considered but seem to match her interest areas. She may intuitively know if the recommended jobs are a good match for her.

Career Exploration

Now that your mentee has a better idea of his interests and skills, the next step is to get him involved with career exploration activities.

Mentor Field Trips: When you and your mentee go anywhere together, observe and discuss the different jobs people have. For example, on a trip to the zoo, you'll see people working as ticket-takers, refreshment and souvenir store clerks, security guards, animal keepers, veterinarians, and managers. Ask your mentee to describe the pros and cons of each job. Does she think it is a job she'd enjoy? Is it a good match for her interests?

Informational interviews: Have your mentee spend 30 minutes interviewing a person working at a job that interests him. He can use the "Informational Interview" form as a guide.

Research: Read about different jobs in books and trade journals or on the Internet.

Career Fairs: Read the paper and watch television ads to learn about career fairs that will be held in your area. Students may be too young to apply for any of the jobs, but they'll learn about the types of jobs available.

Job Shadowing: Following different professionals throughout their workday will provide your mentee with firsthand experience of the work environment and skills required for the job. Two excellent job shadowing websites are www.jobshadow.org and www.virtualjobshadow.com.

Volunteering: Help your mentee find volunteer opportunities in their career interest areas. Check out these websites: Volunteer Match at http://www.volunteermatch.org and www.idealist.org to provide you with information on volunteering.

Extracurricular Activities: Have your mentee join clubs at school and in his community that will give him leadership experience, develop his skills, and help him explore different careers. For example: Scouts, 4-H, YMCA, Boys and Girls Clubs of America, Future Teachers of America, and MESA—Mathematics, Engineering, Science Achievement.

Part-time Jobs: Once your mentee determines a possible career interest, help her find a part-time job that will give her experience in that area.

Career Exploration
Informational Interview

Name of Person Interviewed _____

Company _____ Job Title _____

How did you get started in this career?

What type of training or education is required to do this job?

What are your job responsibilities?

What is a typical workday like?

What are the stressors or difficult parts of your job?

What are the rewards or positive parts of your job?

What is the starting and average salary for this position?

What advice would you give a person entering this field?

Exploring Careers Websites

BLS Career Information. Bureau of Labor Statistics. http://www.bls.gov/k12/

Career Voyages. Department of Labor. http://www.careervoyages.gov/students-main.

Girl Power—Girls at Work. http://www.girlpower.gov/girlarea/sciencetech/jobs/index.htm

Life Works—Office of Science Education. National Institute of Health. http://www.science.education.nih.gov/LifeWorks.nsf/feature/index.htm

NASA Educator Astronaut Program. http://edspace.nasa.gov/

Scientists in Action. U.S. Geological Survey. http://eng.usgs.gov/isb/pubs/booklet/scientists/indexhtml

Small Business Administration's Teen Web Guide. http://www.sba.gov/teens/

The Federal Courtroom. U.S. Department of Justice. http://www.usdoj.gov/usao/eousa/kidspage/index.html

Future State. U.S. Department of State for Youth. http://www.future.state.gov/

Women of NASA. http://quest.arc.nasa.gov/women/intro.html

American Dental Association's Career Resources. http://www.ada.org/public/education/careers/index.asp

Aquarium Careers—Monterey Bay Aquarium. http://www.mbayaq.org/lc/kids-place/kidseq-careers.asp

Careers in Veterinary Medicine. American Veterinary Medical Association. http://www.avma.org/careforanimals/animatedjourney/about vets ...

Discover Engineering. http://www.discoverengineering.org

GetTech.org. www.gettech.org

Girls Go Tech—Careers You Can Count On. www.girlsgotech.org/careers.html

B. POST-SECONDARY EDUCATION

In 1987, the Hudson Institute's *Workforce 2000* research found that by the year 2000, *52% of jobs in the United States would require at least some post-secondary education.* The U.S. Department of Labor's *Learning a Living: A Blueprint for High Performance* reported that "... in many places today, a high school diploma is little more than a certificate of attendance." The research found that the percentage of men with only a high school diploma who could support their family of four above the national poverty level has been decreasing every year.

In other words, if your mentee wants to have a job where she will earn a good salary to provide for herself and her family, she must continue her education after high school graduation. You can help her prepare for post-secondary education by being sure she has a complete high school portfolio documenting her 9th through 12th grade accomplishments.

High School Portfolio

A student came into my office for assistance in May of his senior year, asking for help in filling out a scholarship form. When we came to the section where he was to list his extra-curricular activities, he could not think of anything he had done in his four years of high school. Even after questioning him at length, he basically said that he had gone home every day after school and watched TV.

Competition to get into the college of your choice and for scholarships can be intense. Your mentee needs to keep a record of her high school accomplishments, talents, and skills, so she has the information ready to transfer onto college and scholarship applications. These records can also be used in writing a resume and filling out job applications. If she is like the young man described above, encourage her to become involved in activities she can include in her portfolio. Help her fill out and keep up-to-date her High School Portfolio Record. Use the following tips to be sure she has listed everything she has accomplished:

- *Extra-Curricular Activities:* Include school, church, and community-based activities such as clubs, sports, music, art, 4-H, scouts, etc.
- *Awards, Certificates, and Honors:* Include every recognition given to him by school, church, and community groups.
- *Work and Volunteer Experiences:* This section includes any part-time jobs such as babysitting, mowing lawns, or working at a fast food restaurant, and volunteer work such as helping with community clean-up projects, serving as a Candy Striper at a hospital, or tutoring younger children.
- *Special Skills and Talents:* Include skills such as languages spoken, musical or artistic talents, sign language, and computer programming.

- *Unique Experiences/Special Circumstances:* These might include living or traveling in other countries, coping with a physical handicap, having a single parent and many siblings. List here anything that makes your life experiences different from most of your peers.
- *References:* Applications usually require at least three references that are people who know you well and can attest to your personal qualities and skills. Family members are not to be used as references. Instead, ask teachers, counselors, principals, church or scout leaders, coaches, family friends, or employers.

Help your mentee update his portfolio quarterly and include in his file copies of any awards or certificates he receives.

High School Portfolio Record

Name:

Address:

City, State, Zip Code: _____

Home Phone: _____ Cell Phone: _____ Email: _____

Date of Birth: _____ Place of Birth: _____

Social Security No. _____ Year of Graduation: _____

High School: _____

School Address: _____

Extra-Curricular Activities:

Grade 7:

Grade 8:

Grade 9:

Grade 10:

Grade 11:

Grade 12:

High School Portfolio—Page 2

Awards, Certificates, Honors, Work/Volunteer Experience:

Grade 7:

Grade 8:

Grade 9:

Grade 10:

Grade 11:

Grade 12:

Special Skills and Talents:

High School Portfolio—Page 3

Unique Experiences/Special Circumstances:

References:

1. Name: _____ Title: _____

   Address: _____

   Phone: _____ Email: _____

2. Name: _____ Title: _____

   Address: _____

   Phone: _____ Email: _____

3. Name: _____ Title: _____

   Address: _____

   Phone: _____ Email: _____

Post-Secondary Education Options

An important part of career exploration is finding out what type of training is needed for the jobs your mentee is considering. Go to your state department of education or higher education websites and connect to their directory of post-secondary schools. You will find that there are more schools available than you realized. Finding the school that best meets your mentee's needs and personal preferences is a time-consuming but worthwhile task.

Selecting a Post-Secondary School

Your mentee can begin his school selection process by thinking about these questions:

- What major career area are you considering?
- What type of education is required for this job?
- Do you want to live at home and go to a school close by, or do you want to move to another town or state for school?
- Would you prefer going to a smaller school of about 1,000 to 5,000 students, or would a large campus of more than 5,000 students sound like a better fit?
- Would you be comfortable going to school in a big city or a small rural community?

Once your mentee is able to answer these questions, her search for a post-secondary school will be easier. Help your mentee identify and gather information about schools where she can get the training she needs for her career choice. Information can be obtained from:

- Asking people who work at these jobs where they went to school.
- Checking with the high school's career counselor.
- Reading the vocational, community college, and university brochures he will be receiving in the mail during his junior and senior years.
- Doing Internet searches of schools in the geographical area she wants to locate.
- Going to College Fairs.

Provide your mentee with copies of the *College Search Information* form where she can record what she has learned about each school. On the form, under the Additional Information section, at the bottom of the page, suggest that your mentee write in anything he learned about the school that might help him decide to put the school in his "yes" or "no" piles. Examples might be: high percentage of ethnic minority students, computers provided to every student, or free cable TV in dorm rooms.

Campus Visits

Suggest that your mentee and her family narrow down their list of potential schools to ten or fifteen. These are the schools that your mentee will want to visit in person. Some schools will provide a virtual online tour on their website that may be helpful if a campus visit is not possible. Include the following activities during your campus visits:

- Arrange a guided tour by calling the admissions office.
- Talk to students attending the school. Ask what they like or dislike about the school. What advice do they have for new students?
- Sit in on one or two classes.
- Read the campus newspaper.
- Spend the night in one of the resident halls.
- Eat in the dorm cafeteria.
- Ask about campus security.
- Locate the student health clinic.
- Check out the student center and gymnasium.
- Drive around the town. What is available for weekend entertainment?

Once all the information has been gathered and campuses have been visited, your mentee will need to decide to which schools she will apply.

School Application Process

Your mentee and his family need to select four or five schools that seem to be the best fit for him. Your mentee can use his High School Portfolio to help him fill out the applications. Be sure he fills out the application forms neatly and completely by typing or using a pen with black ink. You can help by proofreading the application and college essay. Be sure he submits the applications and all the required attachments by the deadlines established for each school.

Post-Secondary Expenses

Post-secondary education is expensive. Help your mentee figure out how much it will cost him to attend school each year. Use the following annual budget outline:

School Tuition	$_____
Student Activity Fees	$_____
Books	$_____
Lab Fees	$_____
Computer	$_____
School Supplies	$_____
Housing	$_____
Food	$_____
Medical Insurance	$_____
Transportation	$_____
Telephone	$_____
Household Items	$_____
Clothes	$_____
Entertainment	$_____
Miscellaneous	$_____
Total	$_____

Your mentee's family may discourage him from continuing his education because they don't believe the family can afford it. Share with them the different methods of paying for post-secondary education. Remind them that even if the money has to be borrowed, it is a good investment in terms of the return in salary earnings that additional education and training provides.

Paying for Post-Secondary Education

FAFSA—Free Application for Federal Student Aid: FAFSA provides money for students to attend post-secondary education. Government grants to qualifying individuals do not have to be repaid unless the student drops out of school. Guaranteed student loans must be repaid. If the parent co-signs for the loan, they are liable for paying it back. The FAFSA applications are available in the high school counseling office, at some public libraries, and online at www.fafsa.ed.gov. The application is long and requires a lot of reading. Your mentee and her family may need your help in filling it out.

Work-Study Programs: Many schools have work-study programs that pay students to work part-time on campus. Your mentee needs to check with the school's financial aid office for a work-study application.

Community Service Programs: Service in Americorps or the Peace Corp will provide financial resources for post-secondary education.

Military Service: Your mentee can get a good technical education in the military and have scholarship money available to her when she leaves the military.

Savings Account: Your mentee and his family can check with their bank about opening a tax-free savings account, so they can start saving for college now.

Employer Contributions: Some employers will pay college tuition for their employees who earn above a "C" in college courses.

Scholarships: Scholarship funds awarded to students to pay for post-secondary education do not have to be repaid. The high school counselor will have applications for scholarships available in your area. The websites below will also help your mentee in her scholarship search.

Scholarship Websites
- SRN Express: Scholarship Resource Network Express at http://www.srnexpress.com/index.cfm
- College Scholarships at www.college-scholarships.com/
- The Scholarship Page! at www.scholarship-page.com/
- FRESCH! Free Scholarship Search at www.freschinfo.com/
- FastWeb! at http://fastweb.monster.com/
- ESF: Education Services Foundation at www.esfweb.com/
- Easy Aid at www.easyaid.com/
- Collegiate Funding at www.collegiatefunding.com/
- College Money at www.collegemoney.com/
- College Funds at www.collegefunds.net/
- College Connection Scholarships at www.collegescholarships.com/

College Search Information

Name of School _____

Address _____

Admissions Phone Number _____ Website _____

School Is: Private or Public   Number of Students: _____
School Is Accredited: Yes or No   Average Class Size: _____
Graduation Rate: _____   Job Placement Rate: _____
Tuition / Semester: $_____   Cost of Books/Fees: $ _____
Housing Costs: $_____   Travel Home Costs: $_____

Types of Financial Aid Provided: _____
_____

Services Offered:
____ On-campus Housing
____ Library
____ Computer Lab
____ Health Clinic
____ Counseling Services
____ Career Services
____ Student Support Services
____ Tutoring
____ Job Placement Services
____ Other _____

Clubs / Activities:
____ Student Government
____ Sports: intramurals and school teams
____ Music, Dance, Drama
____ Career-specific Clubs
____ Sororities and Fraternities
____ Service Clubs
____ Other _____

Additional Information:

Post-Secondary Education Application Checklist

Junior Year

____ Take college preparation classes. Study hard to get good grades.

____ Get involved in extra-curricular activities.

____ Take the PSAT/NMSQT (National Merit Scholarship Qualifying Test).

____ Take ACT/SAT college entrance exams.

____ If you are in Advanced Placement classes, take the AP exams in May.

____ Develop a filing system to organize college materials that come in the mail or that you pick up at College Fairs or print from the Internet.

____ Participate in career exploration activities. Start to narrow down your career choices.

____ Update your portfolio information.

Senior Year

____ Review your collected college materials. Narrow your college choices down to 10 or 15 schools.

____ Schedule and begin visiting your chosen colleges.

____ Retake SAT/ACT tests to improve your scores.

____ Select 5 schools you'd like to apply to. Begin filling out the application forms. Get the applications mailed in by the deadlines for each school.

____ Work on your college essay. Have several people proofread the essay before you send it in with the applications.

____ Approach teachers, family friends, and employers to ask for a Letter of Reference. Ask them 3 to 4 weeks before the application deadlines to give them enough time to write the letter.

____ Create a filing system for your application copies.

____ Request financial aid and scholarship information from the colleges you have applied to.

____ In January, begin filling out FAFSA forms. Ask your parents to do their income taxes in February, as a copy has to be attached to the FAFSA.

____ Search for and apply for scholarships.

____ Send thank-you notes to people who wrote letters and helped you with your college search and application process.

____ Send an acceptance letter to the college you have chosen to attend.

____ Study hard all year. Get good grades. Celebrate your success!

C. EMPLOYABILITY SKILLS

Whether your mentee goes on to post-secondary education or enters the workforce immediately after high school graduation, he needs to learn basic employability skills to assist him in finding a good job. He needs to know:

- What skills today's employers need.
- How to write a good resume.
- How to fill out job applications.
- How to do well on job interviews.

21st Century Job Skills

The U.S. Labor Department, in their SCANS America 2000 report, *Learning a Living: A Blueprint for High Performance*, identifies foundation skills and workplace competencies that employers require of their work force.

Foundation Skills:

- BASIC SKILLS: reading, writing, mathematics, speaking, and listening.
- THINKING SKILLS: the ability to learn, to reason, to think creatively, to make decisions, and to solve problems.
- PERSONAL QUALITIES: individual responsibility, self-esteem and self-management, sociability, and integrity.

Workplace Competencies:

- RESOURCES: Employees know how to allocate time, money, materials, space, and staff.
- INTERPERSONAL SKILLS: Employees can work on teams, teach others, serve customers, lead, negotiate, and work well with people from culturally diverse backgrounds.
- INFORMATION: Employees can acquire and evaluate data, organize and maintain files, interpret and communicate, and use computers to process information.
- SYSTEMS: Employees understand social, organizational, and technological systems; they can monitor and correct performance, and they can design or improve systems.

- TECHNOLOGY: Employees can select equipment and tools, apply technology to specific tasks, and maintain and troubleshoot equipment.

Your mentee will be competitive in the job market when she can demonstrate on her resume that she has mastered and can use these required basic skills and workplace competencies on the job.

Developing a Resume

A resume is a short outline that summarizes who you are, the kind of position you want, skills you've mastered, accomplishments you have made, and a listing of your education, training, and previous work experience. A resume is your first introduction to a prospective employer. Companies will use your resume as a screening tool to determine whether or not you will be given a job interview.

Effective, professional-looking resumes are:
- One to two pages long
- Concise and accurate
- Typed in a 12 point non-decorative font
- Printed on 8 1/2" x 11" paper
- Typed on good quality white or off-white paper
- Printed on one side of paper only
- Easy to read

Use the sample resume that follows as a guide when you help your mentee write her resume. Resumes are divided into the following basic sections:

Introductory Heading: Your contact information goes at the top of the resume and contains:

- Your full legal name (printed in bold)
- Permanent mailing address
- City, state, zip code
- (Area code) telephone number
- Cell phone number
- Email address

Career Objective: A career objective states the level of position you are applying for, a one or two word description of the type of business or industry, and major strengths you bring to the job. For example:

Level of Position: Entry level
Type of Industry: Hospitality Industry
Your Strengths: Excellent customer service and organizational skills
Career Objective: To obtain an entry-level position in the hospitality industry where I can use my organizational skills and customer service experience.

Education: List your most recent education first. State the name of the school, location, year attended, degree earned, and specific skills you learned that can be used on the job for which you are applying.

Work Experience: Starting with your present or most current job, list the employer, your position, years of employment, major job responsibilities, and accomplishments.

Skills: List skills related to the job such as computer software you can use, equipment you can operate, languages you speak, and artistic talents.

Activities: List extracurricular, community, and volunteer activities you have been involved in that help demonstrate your qualifications for the job for which you are applying.

"References Available Upon Request": Add this phrase at the bottom of your resume. Have a separate page listing at least three personal or work-related references that you can give to the employer upon their request.

The High School Portfolio Record that your mentee has filled out and continually updated will make it easy for him to develop his resume. You can help by proofreading his resume for spelling and grammatical errors.

Sample Resume

Natasha F. Salas
123 Yourstreet Drive
Yourtown, CO 12345
(123) 456-7890
Youremail@rmii.com

Career Objective

To obtain an entry-level position in the hospitality industry where I can use my organizational skills, college training, and customer service experience.

Education

Columbia Community College, Yourtown, CO, Associates Degree, 2005
Major: Restaurant Management.

Yourtown High School, Yourtown, CO, High School Diploma, 2003
Graduated in top ten percent of my class.

Work Experience

Hostess, Brown's Family Restaurant, Yourtown, CO, 2003 to 2004
Hired, scheduled, and supervised wait staff, greeted and seated customers, operated cash register, conducted front-of-the-house inventory, and did informal customer satisfaction assessments.

Wait Staff, Garcia's Restaurant, Yourtown, CO, 2002 to 2003
Waited on customers, delivered food, operated cash register.

Skills

Bilingual in English and Spanish; certified in food safety; can operate computerized cash registers; knowledgeable in restaurant management software and basic principles of accounting; excellent customer service skills.

Activities

President, High School International Students Club
Taught Spanish in After-School Program at YourTown Elementary

References Available Upon Request

Cover Letter

When you send resumes to potential employers, always send a cover letter with the resume. Cover letters should be brief, neatly typed on good quality 8½" x 11" paper, and addressed specifically to the company to which you are applying. Use the sample cover letter as a guide and follow these steps:

1. *Inside Address:* Your street address, city/state/zip code, and the date you are mailing the letter.

2. *Company Address:* The name of the person (if you know it) you are writing to, the person's job title, company, and company address.

3. *Greeting*: Dear Mr. or Ms. followed by the person's last name to whom you are writing. If you don't have a specific person's name, write Dear Sir or Madam.

4. *Paragraph One:* State the position you are applying for and where you learned about the job opening.

5. *Paragraph Two:* Highlight the skills and experiences you have that qualify you for this job.

6. *Paragraph Three*: Request a job interview.

7. *Thank You*: End with a brief thank you for their time and consideration statement.

8. *Closing:* Sincerely, skip three or four lines to leave a space for your signature, and type in your name as it appears on the resume.

Sample Cover Letter

123 Yourstreet Drive
Yourtown, CO 12345
June 20, 2005

Ms. Maria Nguyen
Manager
The Asian-Pacific Gourmet Restaurant
7000 Main Street
Seattle, WA 12345

Dear Ms. Nugyen:

I am submitting this letter of application and my resumé for the position of main dining room hostess that was advertised on your website.

I have recently graduated with my associate's degree in restaurant management from Columbia Community College. I am now living in Seattle and am available immediately for full-time employment. I believe I have the training and work experience that qualifies me for this position.

I would appreciate the opportunity to meet with you and interview for the hostess position. Please call me at your convenience at the phone number listed on my resume.

Thank you for your consideration.

Sincerely,

Natasha F. Salas

Enc.

References

Employers will ask you for the names and contact information of three to five references—people who are familiar with your work and personal qualities. They will call or write your references to inquire as to how they know you and their observations of your work skills, strengths, and weaknesses. Obviously, you will ask only those people who think highly of you if they would be willing to be a job reference for you. References might be a co-worker, supervisor, class instructor, customer, or family friend. On a separate sheet of paper, with your name and contact information typed at the top, list the name, title, company, address, phone number, and email address of each of your references. Have your Personal References list available to give to potential employers during job interviews.

Filling Out Job Applications

A personnel manager once told a group of students I worked with that if the job application was sloppy, she wouldn't even read it. Instead, she just put it in her circular file—the wastebasket.

Many companies will ask applicants to fill out a job application. Your mentee's High School Portfolio Record, Resume, and Personal References list will contain most of the information he needs to fill out the application. Share these job application pointers with your mentee to ensure that his application does not end up in the "circular file."

- Have a copy of your High School Portfolio record, resume, personal references list, social security card, and driver's license with you; you'll need this information to help you fill-out the job application.
- Read all the instructions before you begin to fill-out the application.
- Use a black pen and write as neatly as possible.
- Take whiteout with you in case you need to correct a mistake.
- Do not fold, bend, or wrinkle the application.
- Don't leave any question blank. If the question does not apply to you, write "not applicable" or "n/a."
- Answer the questions truthfully.
- Be sure the information on your resume and the application are the same.
- Proofread your application carefully before you submit it.
- Ask the employer when you can expect to hear back from them. If you do not hear back from them within the timeframe they provided, give them a call to check on the status of your application.

Job Interviewing

The job interview helps the employer determine if you are the kind of person they want working for them. Some companies may have you go through three or four interviews with different people—the initial screener, personnel director, supervisor of the vacant position, and the manager or owner.

Employers know that people can exaggerate or put false information on their resumes or job applications, and their personal references may be reluctant to say anything negative about the job applicant. However, when the interviewer has you in her office, she can personally assess your appearance, social manners, communication skills, and appropriateness of your responses to interview questions. Help your mentee have a successful job interview by reviewing the following tips with her.

Get Prepared
- Find out information about the company. Read their website; talk to people who work there; collect and read the company's informational brochures.
- Be familiar with the job description and other requirements the company has for their employees.
- Be clear on how this job relates to your career objectives.
- Take your resume, list of references, driver's license or photo I.D., and social security card.
- Prepare answers to the most frequently asked interview questions.
- Practice interviewing with a family member or friend.
- Select appropriate clothes for the interview, using what the company's employees usually wear to work as a standard.
- Arrive at the interview at least 10 to 15 minutes early.

First Impressions

Sara showed up for the job interview with green-streaked hair, earrings in her eyebrows, black polish on her nails, flip flops on her feet, gum in her mouth, skirt above her knees, and smelling of cigarette smoke.

Juan showed up for the job interview in nice khaki slacks, shirt tucked in, polished shoes, no jewelry except a watch and his class ring, and a well-groomed haircut.

Who do you think will be hired? Why?

The impression you make on the receptionist and interviewer as you walk through the front door is very important. They want employees who will represent their company well, maintain company standards in appearance, and look like a person with whom their clients would feel comfortable working. When you go to the interview, take extra care with your appearance:

- Arrive early enough to go to the restroom to check on your appearance. Don't forget to check your teeth. Food stuck in your teeth is very unattractive.
- Wear clean, pressed clothes that meet the company's clothing standards.
- Wear polished shoes.
- Have neat, clean hair and fingernails (No outlandish nail polish).
- Wear only conservative, professional-looking jewelry. No piercings.
- No chewing gum, candy, or cigarettes.
- No cologne or perfume.
- Only light, professional-looking make-up.

Interviews can be stressful.
Looking your best gives you more self-confidence.

Interview Etiquette

From the moment you walk through the company's front door and up to the receptionist's desk, your personality and social skills will be on review. Are you the type of person with whom they want to spend eight hours a day, five days a week? Are you friendly? Do you have good manners? When applicants' skills and work experience are similar, the interviewer will hire the person whose personality is a better fit for their work environment. Your mentee can impress the interviewer by practicing the following workplace etiquette:

- Smile! Have a facial expression that communicates to people that you are friendly and pleased to meet them.
- Make eye contact. Look directly at the person to whom you are speaking.
- Stand up when you are introduced to someone.
- Introduce yourself immediately. Tell the other person your first and last names and a statement about who you are. "Hello. I'm Natasha Salas, and I'm here to interview for your main dining room hostess position."
- Shake hands firmly with the other person.
- Repeat the other person's name when he introduces himself to help you remember it. "Mr. Johnson, "I'm pleased to meet you."
- Wait until you are invited before you sit down.
- Sit up straight. Don't fidget.
- Don't cross your arms and legs. This position sends a message that you are closed-off and unreceptive.
- Put your briefcase and handbag on the floor instead of in your lap.
- Don't talk too slowly, quickly, softly, or too loudly.
- Try to appear relaxed and confident.

Frequently Asked Questions

There are standard questions your mentee may be asked during her job interview.

Thinking about her answers in advance will give her a competitive edge and help her feel more confident during the interview. Help her prepare appropriate answers to some of these questions:

- "Tell me about yourself." Answer with four or five things you want the interviewer to know about your background and skills that qualify you to do the job for which you are interviewing.

- "Why do you want to work here?" Explain what you know about the company's products and services and why you think their company is a good fit for you.

- "What are your career goals?" Describe how the career objective you have written on your resume relates to the position for which you are applying. Let them know you are interested in increasing your skills and growing professionally within the company.

- "What is your greatest accomplishment?" Talk about something you did at work that produced good results for your employer or a school project that was productive and helpful to others.

- "Tell me about a stressful work situation you experienced. How did you handle it?" Relate an incident using the facts of the situation without being too negative about anyone else involved. Describe what you did to help yourself and others resolve the situation to the best possible outcome.

- "Why should we hire you?" Using tasks listed on the job description, discuss how your skills, training, and work experience make you highly qualified for the position.

After your mentee has written out his responses to these and other potential questions, have him practice in a mock interview with you as the interviewer. Provide him with helpful feedback about his appearance, social manners, communication style, and demeanor.

Questions to Ask the Interviewer

During the job interview, your mentee will have an opportunity to ask questions that have not already been answered by the interviewer and that might influence your mentee's decision to accept or turn down any job offer that might be made. Discuss with your mentee what additional information she would like to know about the company and help her write out questions to ask. A few questions she might consider are:

- Could you provide me with a more detailed job description? What kinds of equipment will I be using? How much training will I receive?
- What types of benefits does the company offer employees? Do you provide health insurance or a retirement program?
- Would there be opportunities for advancement? Would it be possible to eventually move into a management or supervisory position?
- When do you hope to make a hiring decision? When can I expect to hear from you?

Ensuring Continued Success

Explain to your mentee that getting the job is only the first step to continued success. Employers will expect their workers to:

- Be dependable and reliable, following through on tasks without the need for constant supervision.
- Be punctual, arriving at work and returning from lunch and breaks on time.
- Do their jobs consistently well.
- Be a good member of the work team.

To earn promotions, ensure job security during employee layoffs, and to know your supervisor will give you a good reference when you move on to other jobs, your mentee will want to work hard and be an excellent employee.

UNIT SIX: BIBLIOGRAPHY

4 Girls Health. "Your Future—Looking Ahead." http://www.4girls.gov/future/discover.htm. (accessed 5/10/05)

America's Promise: The Alliance for Youth http://www.americaspromise.org/youth/linked/index.cfm. (accessed 8/6/05)

Bellevue University Career Service. "Using References Effectively In Your Job Search." http://academic.bellevue.edu/%7Ecareer/Reference.htm. (accessed 5/10/05)

Bureau of Labor Statistics. "What Interests You?" http://www.bls.gov/k12/. (accessed 5/10/05)

Bureau of Labor Statistics. "Occupational Outlook Handbook."http://stats.bls.gov/oco/. (accessed 5/11/05)

"Career Exploration: The Personal Side of Work." http://www.jobprofiles.org. (accessed 5/11/05)

Career Planning. "Job Seeking Skills Checklist" "Employment Applications" "Keeping a Job" "Growing on the Job" "Resumes" "Career Planning" "Self-Assessment" http://www.soicc.state.nc.us/soicc/planning/c3a.htm. (accessed 5/11/05)

Casey Family Programs. (2004) "It's My Life: Employment." www.casey.org.

CollegeBoard.com. "Find a College."http://www.collegeboard.com/csearch/. (accessed 8/6/05)

Connecticut Department of Labor. (2001) "Employment Interviewing." http://www.ctdol.state.ct.us/progsupt/jobsrvce/intervie.htm. (accessed 5/11/05)

First Gov for Kids. "Careers—Government Sites." http://www.kids.gov/k_careers.htm. (accessed 5/10/05)

Hansen, Katherine. "Research Companies and Careers Through Job Shadowing." Quintessential Careers: Your Job Search Starts Here website. http://www.quintcareers.com/job_shadowing.html. (accessed 8/6/05)

Hansen, Katherine. "How to Make the Most of Your Campus Visit."Quintessential Careers: Your Job Search Starts Here website. http://www.quintcareers.com/campus_visit.html. (accessed 8/6/05)

Hansen, Randall S. "Developing a Strategic Vision for Your Career Plan." Quintessential Careers: Your Job Search Starts Here website. http://quintcareers.com/career_plan.html. (accessed 5/11/05)

Hansen, Randall S. "The Importance of the High School Junior Year." Quintessential Careers: Your Job Search Starts Here website. http://www.quintcareers.com/high-school_junior_year.html. (accessed 8/6/05)

Hansen, Randall S. "College Admissions Do's and Don'ts. "Quintessential Careers: Your Job Search Starts Here website. http://www.quintcareers.com/college_admissions-dos-donts.html. (accessed 8/6/05)

Hansen, Randall S. "College-Bound High School Senior Planning Calendar." Quintessential Careers: Your Job Search Starts Here website. http://www.quintcareers.com/college_application_timeline.html. (accessed 8/6/05)

Hansen, Randall S. "Choosing a College that's Right for You." Quintessential Careers: Your Job Search Starts Here website. http://www.quintcareers.com/choosing_a_college.html. (accessed 8/6/05)

The High School Graduate.com. "College Bound: Surviving Your College Search." http://www.thehighschoolgraduate.com/editorial/Ussearch.htm. (accessed 7/14/05)

Job Shadowing 2005. www.jobshadow.org/ (accessed 8/8/05)

JobWeb.com. "Add Up Your Qualifications." http://www.jobweb.com/resources/library/Interviews/Add_up_your_qua_266_I.htm. (accessed 5/11/05)

JobWeb.com. "Resumes & Interviews. http://www.jobweb.com/Resumes_Interviews/default.htm. (accessed 5/11/05)

Maryland Careers. "References: Strategy for Job Seekers." http://www.marylandcareers.org/referencesI.html. (accessed 5/11/05)

Miller, Carol and VanDecar, Elena. (2004). *Parenting for Academic Success.* Denver, CO: Latin American Research and Service Agency.

O'Rourke, Suzanne and Moore, Dorothy. "Career Exploration." http://csis.pace.edu/schools/nr/sorourke/sorlesson.htm. (accessed 5/11/05)

Ramsey, Lydia. "Etiquette for Meeting People in Business." http://www.hodu.com/meeting-etiquette.shtml. (accessed 6/15/05)

Tanabe, Gen & Kelly. "Four Steps To Getting Perfect College Recommendations. Quintessential Careers: Your Job Search Starts Here website. http://www.quintcareers.com/college_recommendations.html. (accessed 8/6/05)

Tanabe, Gen & Kelly. "Acing Your College Interview." Quintessential Careers: Your Job Search Starts Here website. http://www.quintcareers.com/college_interview.html. (accessed 8/6/05)

Thomas More College. "Job Search." http://www2.thomasmore.edu/career/job_interview_quiz. (accessed 5/11/05)

U.S. Department of Education. "Especially for Students." http://www.ed.gov/students/landing.jhtml. (accessed 5/10/05)

U.S. Department of Labor. (1998). *Learning a Living: A Blueprint for High Performance: A Scans Report for America 2000.*

Virtual Job Shadow: Interactive Career Exploration. www.virtualjobshadow.com/. (accessed 8/8/05)

Hudson Institute. (1987) *Workforce 2000.*

Yate, Martin. "Resumes Win Interviews, But References Win Job Offers. Wall Street Journal Executive Career Site. Http://www.careerjournal.com/jobhunting/resumes/19980828-yate.html. (accessed 5/11/05)